Emma Farrarons is a French illustrator and
graphic designer. Born on the island of Cebu in the Philippines,
Emma grew up in Paris.

She was trained in illustration at the Edinburgh
College of Art and l'École nationale supérieure des Arts
Décoratifs. Having completed a textile and printmaking course at
Capellagården school in Sweden, she has developed a particular
love of pattern and fabric print and is inspired by French,
Scandinavian and Japanese design. She illustrates and
designs books, posters and stationery.

When she is not drawing and designing, Emma
enjoys cookery, sewing, travel and practising mindfulness.
She lives in London with her Danish husband.

Share your creations using **#mindfulnesscolouringbook**
Visit the Mindfulness Colouring website at
www.mindfulnesscolouring.com
See more of Emma's work at **www.emmafarrarons.com**

Also by Emma Farrarons

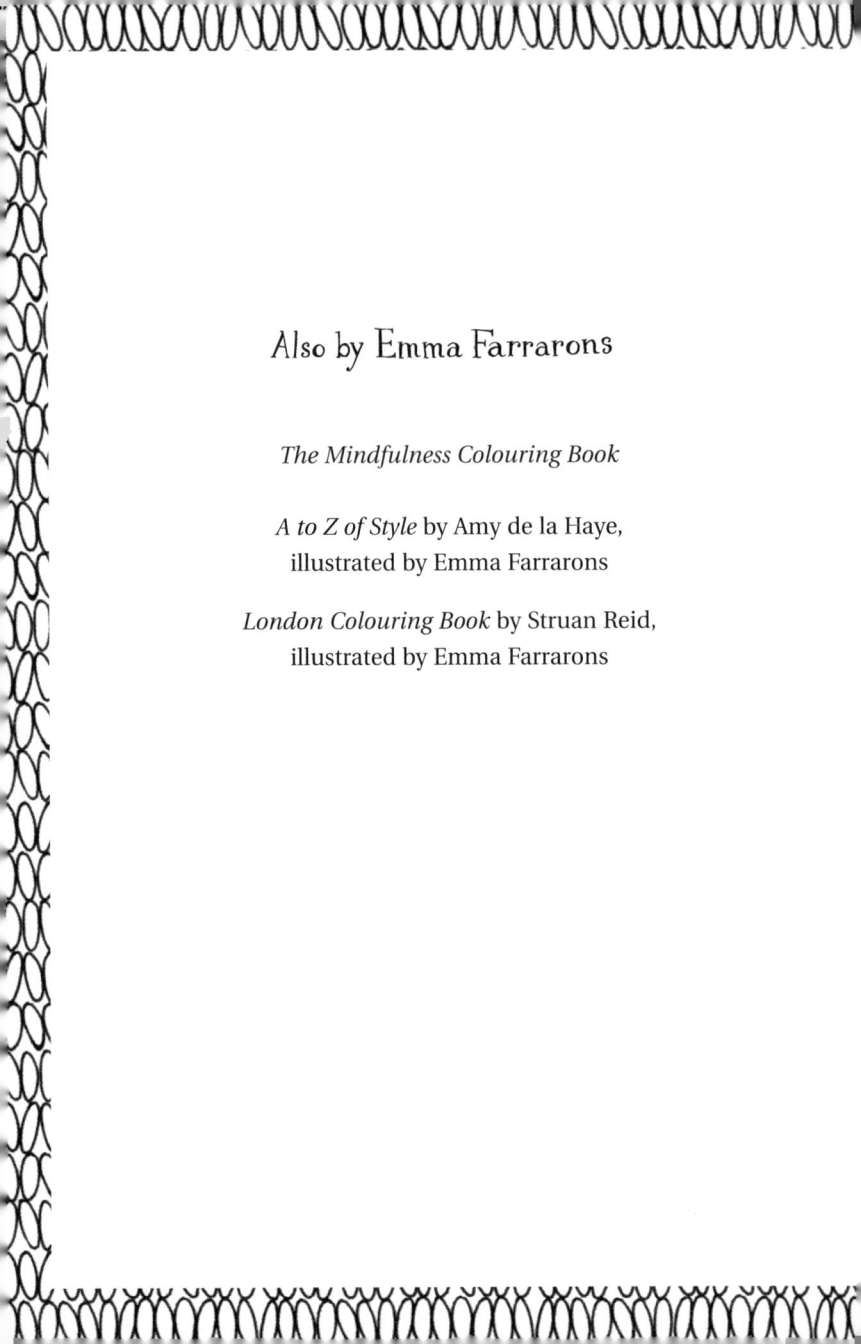

The Mindfulness Colouring Book

A to Z of Style by Amy de la Haye,
illustrated by Emma Farrarons

London Colouring Book by Struan Reid,
illustrated by Emma Farrarons

More
MINDFULNESS COLOURING

More anti-stress art therapy for busy people

Emma Farrarons

B⊛XTREE

First published 2015 by Boxtree
an imprint of Pan Macmillan
20 New Wharf Road, London N1 9RR
Associated companies throughout the world
www.panmacmillan.com

ISBN 978-0-7522-6573-5

Copyright © Emma Farrarons 2015

The right of Emma Farrarons to be identified as the
author of this work has been asserted by her in accordance
with the Copyright, Designs and Patents Act 1988.

All rights reserved. No part of this publication may be reproduced,
stored in a retrieval system, or transmitted, in any form, or by any means
(electronic, mechanical, photocopying, recording or otherwise)
without the prior written permission of the publisher.

Pan Macmillan does not have any control over, or any responsibility for,
any author or third party websites referred to in or on this book.

1 3 5 7 9 8 6 4 2

A CIP catalogue record for this book is available from the British Library.

Printed in Italy

This book is sold subject to the condition that it shall not, by way of
trade or otherwise, be lent, hired out, or otherwise circulated without
the publisher's prior consent in any form of binding or cover other than
that in which it is published and without a similar condition including
this condition being imposed on the subsequent purchaser.

Visit **www.panmacmillan.com** to read more about all our books
and to buy them. You will also find features, author interviews and
news of any author events, and you can sign up for e-newsletters
so that you're always first to hear about our new releases.

For Cindy Chan

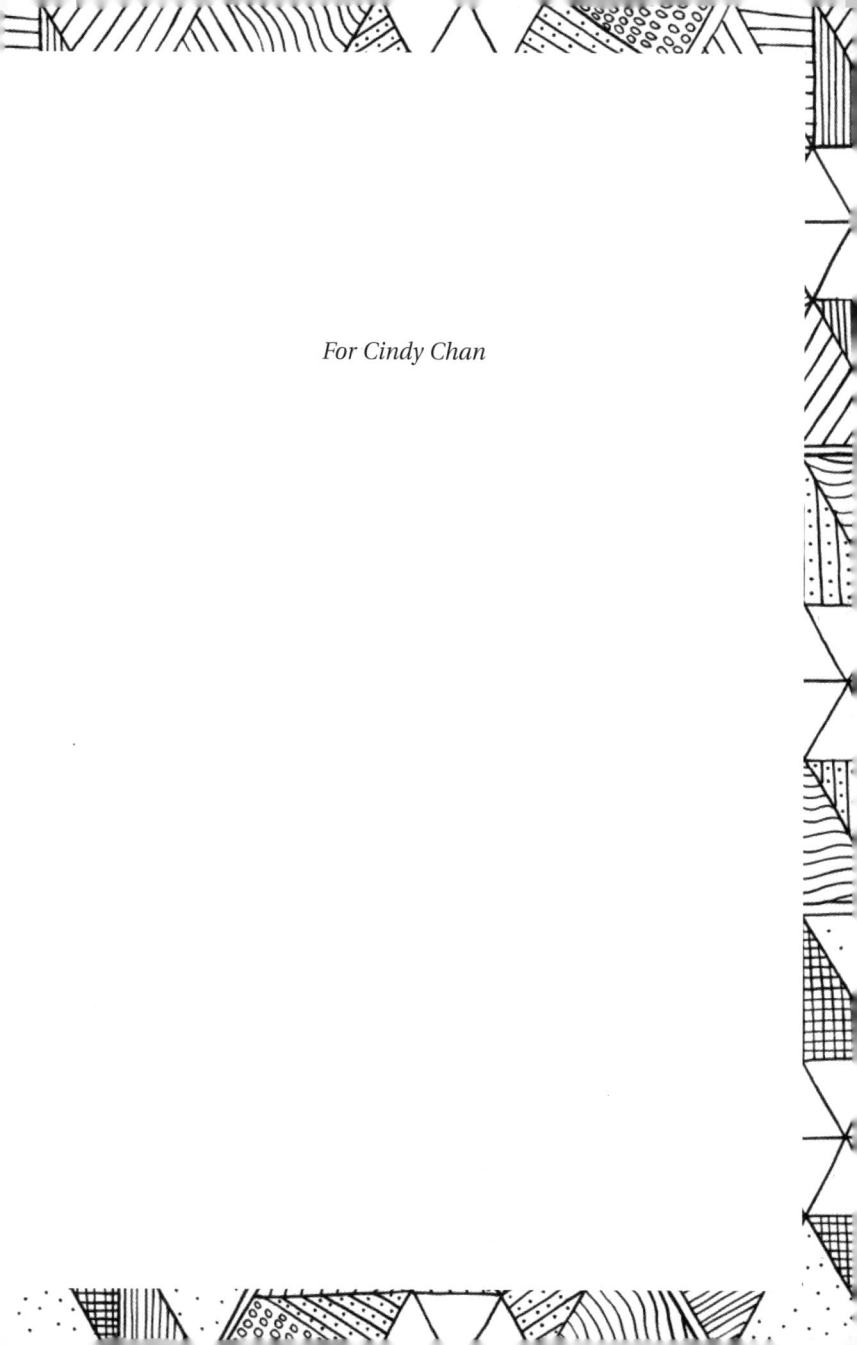

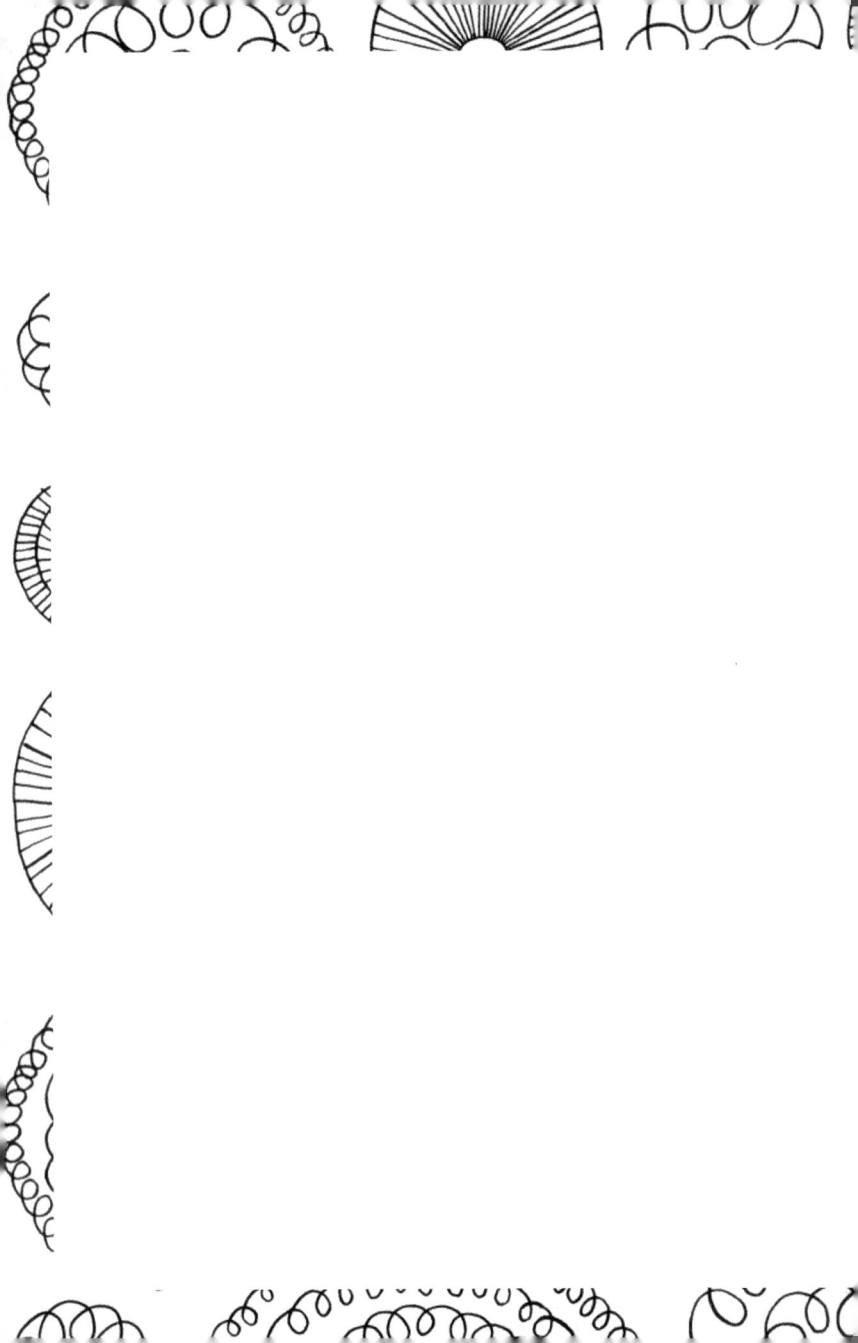

INTRODUCTION

Modern life can be very challenging at times. We rush around trying to get everything done: looking after our homes and families, keeping on top of our workloads, not to mention the seemingly never-ending texts, calls and emails we receive throughout the day. Sometimes even trying to make time to see our friends and enjoy our favourite pastimes can feel stressful. But we now know that taking a moment to pause and be mindful can dramatically improve our well-being, making us feel calmer, more at peace with our emotions and, as a result, more capable of dealing with the demands of the day.

Being mindful is about paying attention to the present moment, clearing your mind of distractions and focusing on simply being. Pretty much any activity, done right, can be an exercise in mindfulness – sitting on the bus, brushing your teeth or simply breathing in and out. But the act of colouring in – carefully and attentively filling a page with colour, the feel of the pencil in your hand as you meditate on the beauty of the illustration – is particularly suited to mindful meditation.

This second book of mindfulness colouring provides the perfect opportunity to take a moment to be mindful. Let the intricate patterns and charming scenes inspire your creativity and relax your mind. Whatever you are doing, wherever you are, we hope you will enjoy taking the time to colour in, de-stress and be mindful.

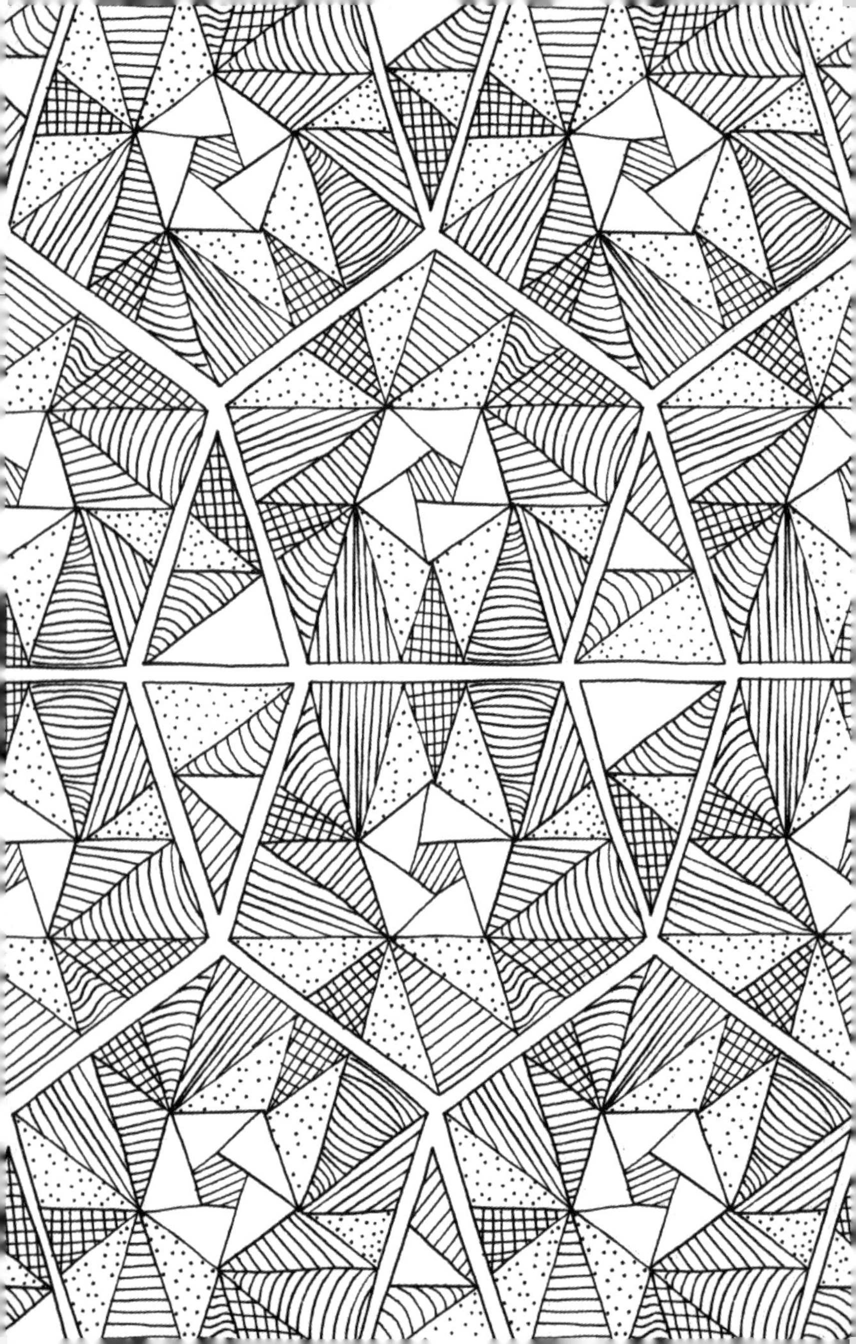

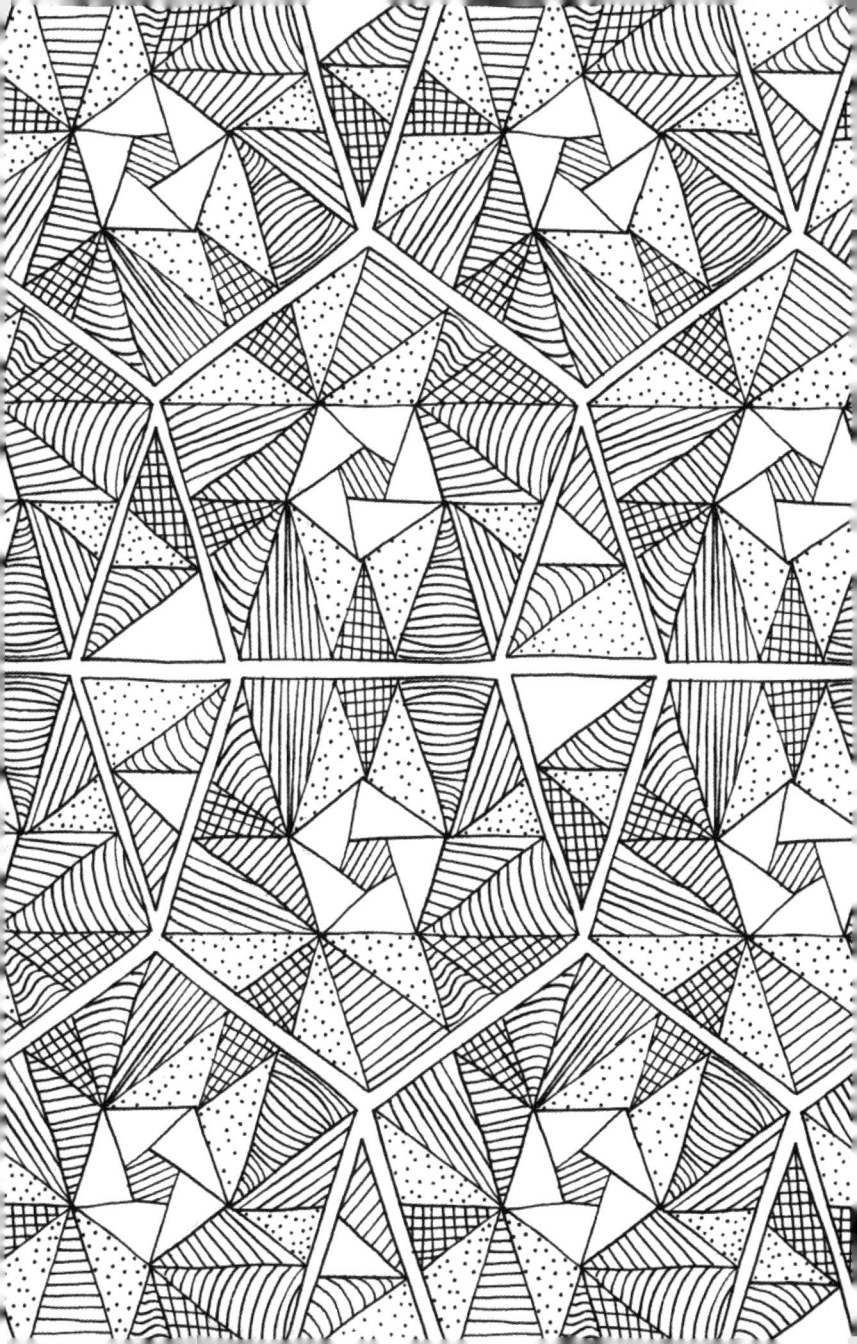

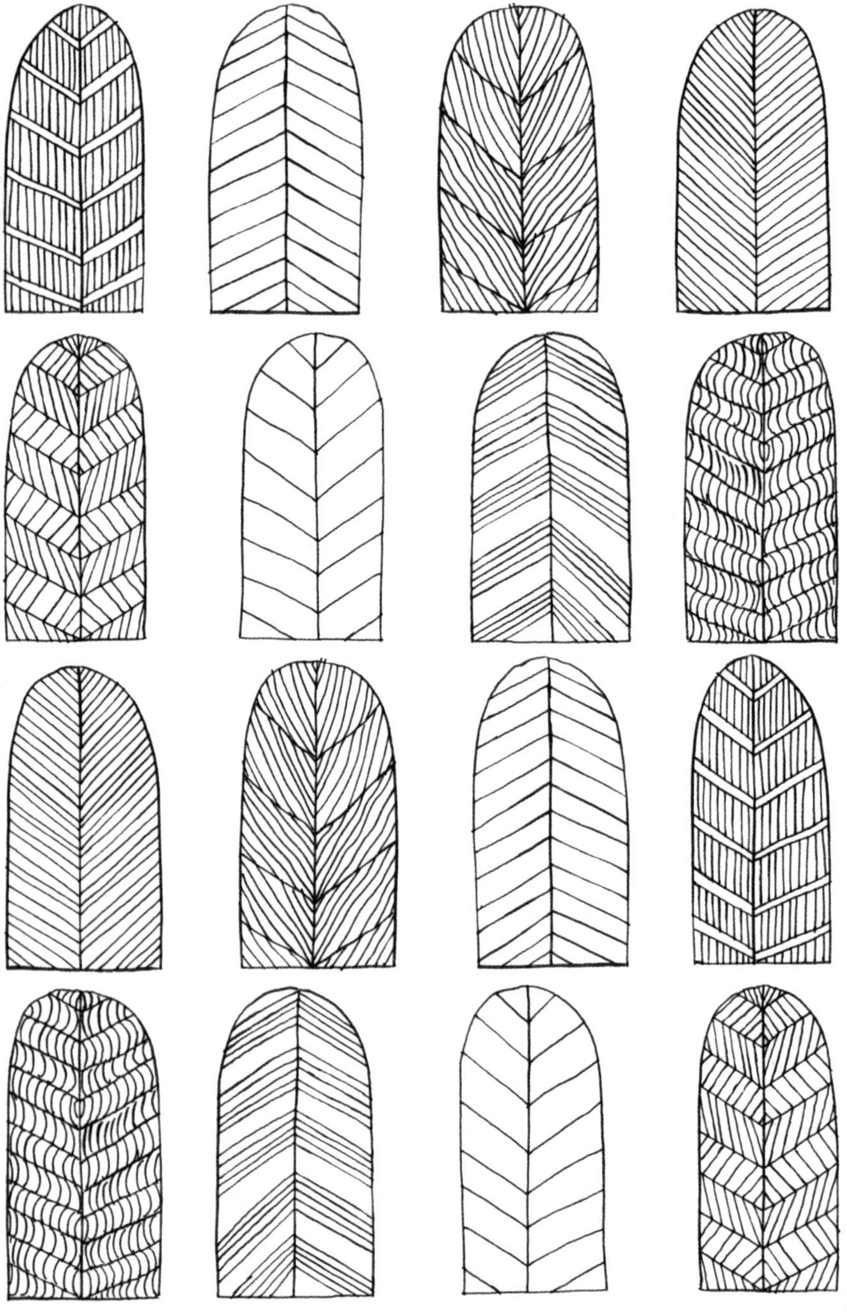

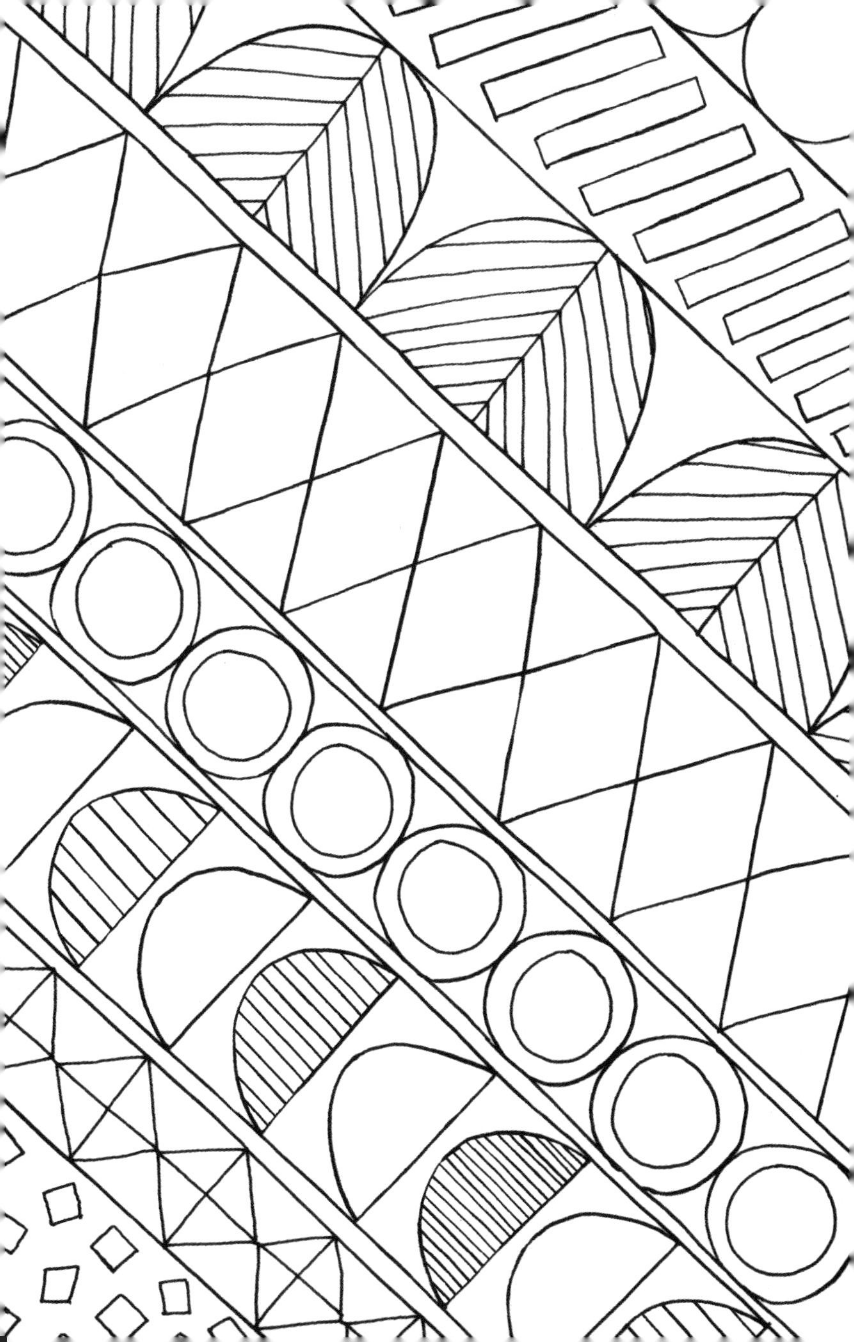

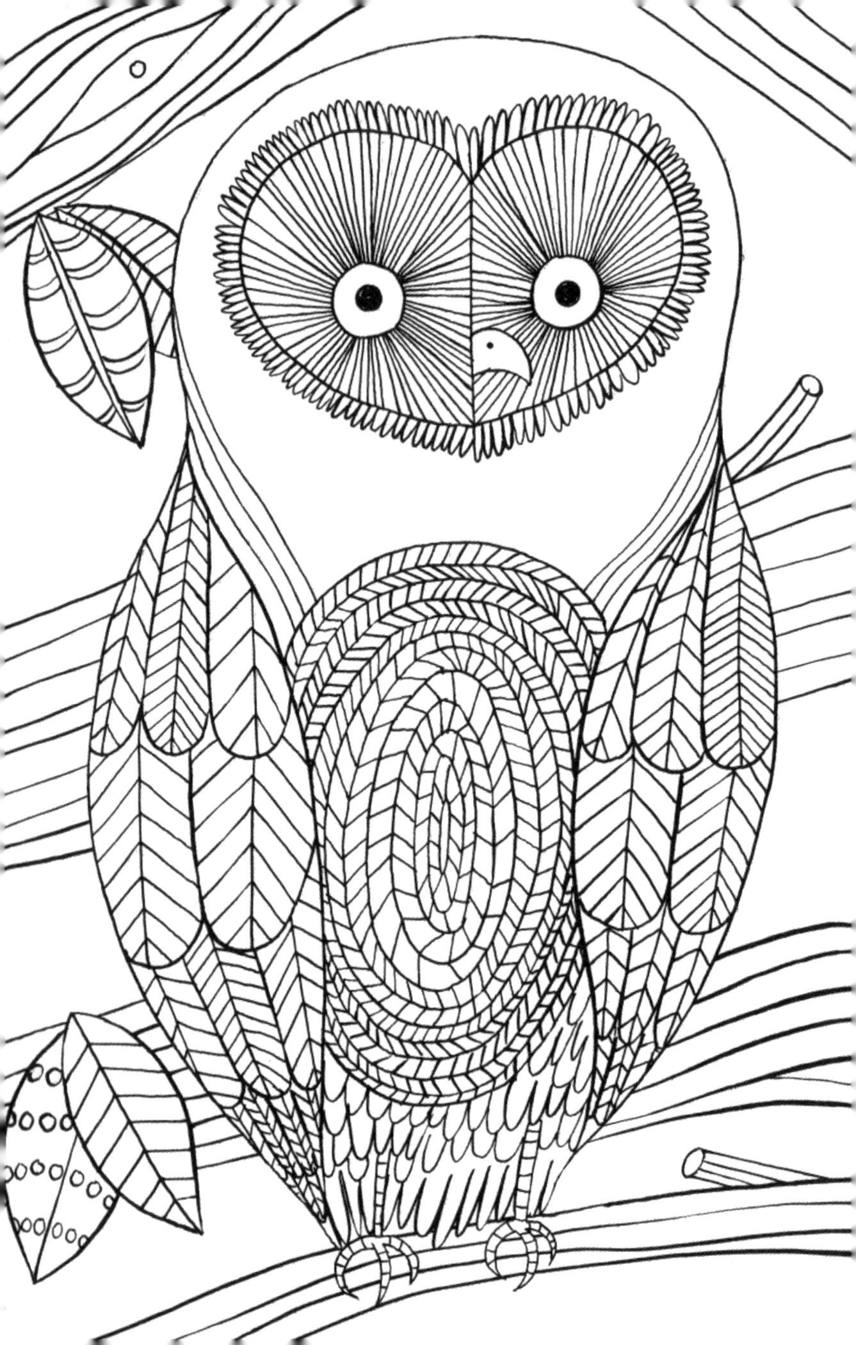

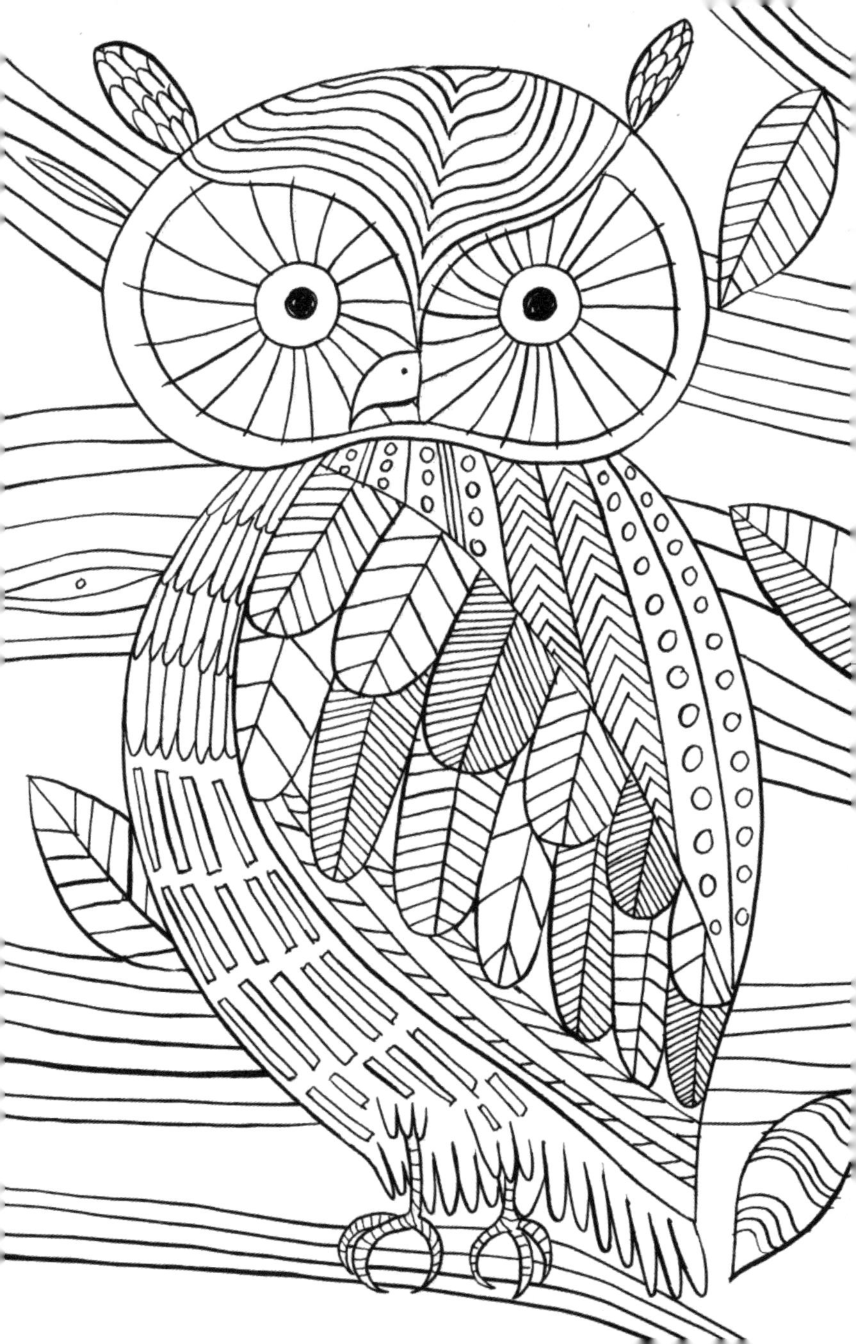

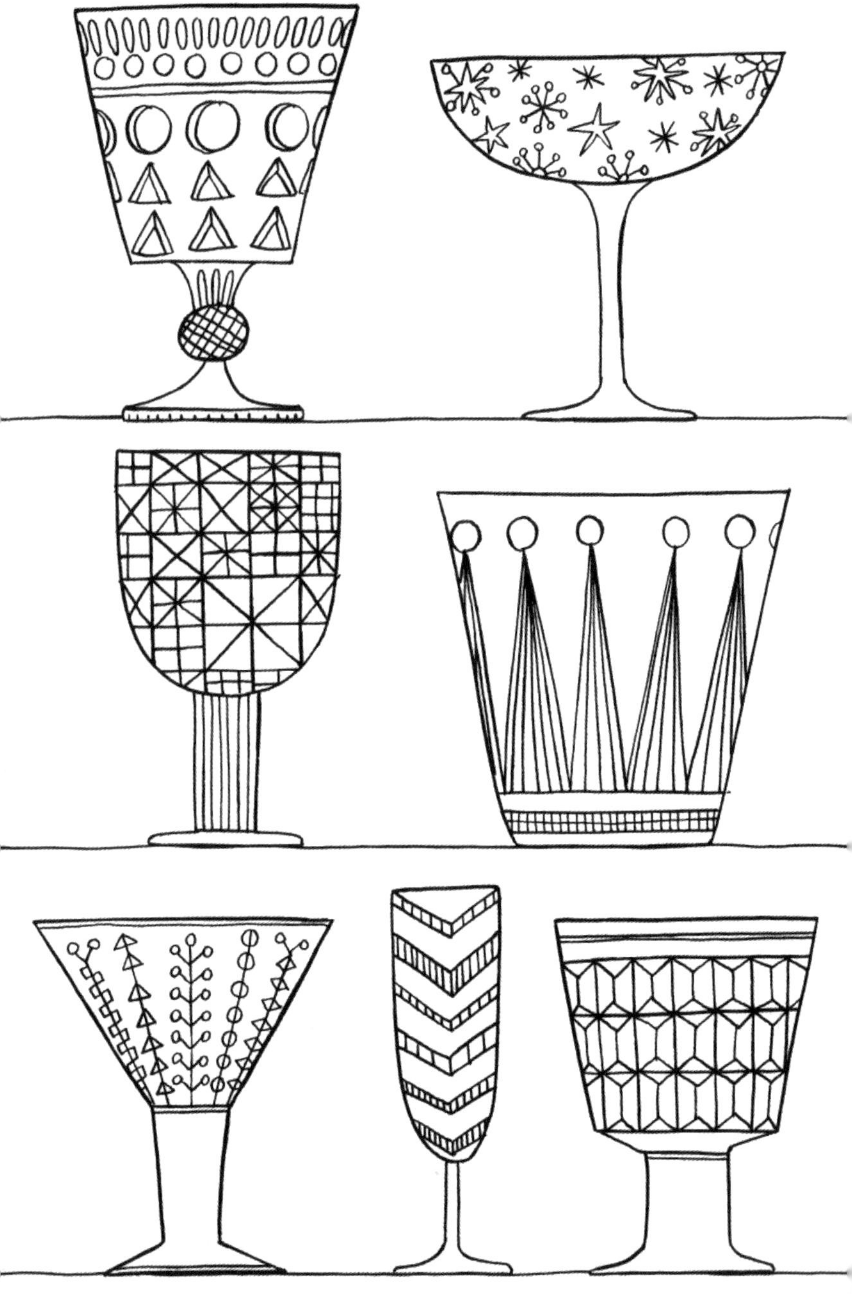

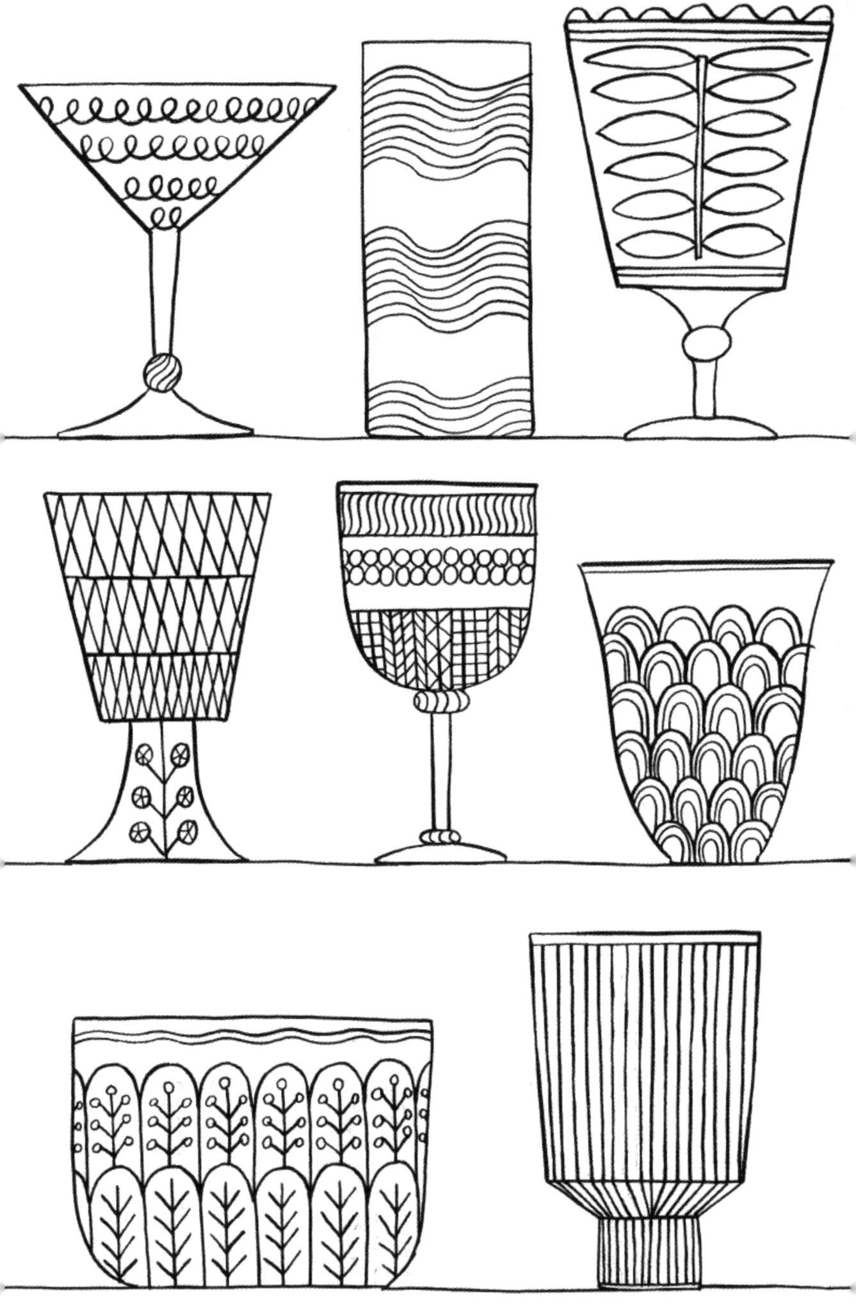

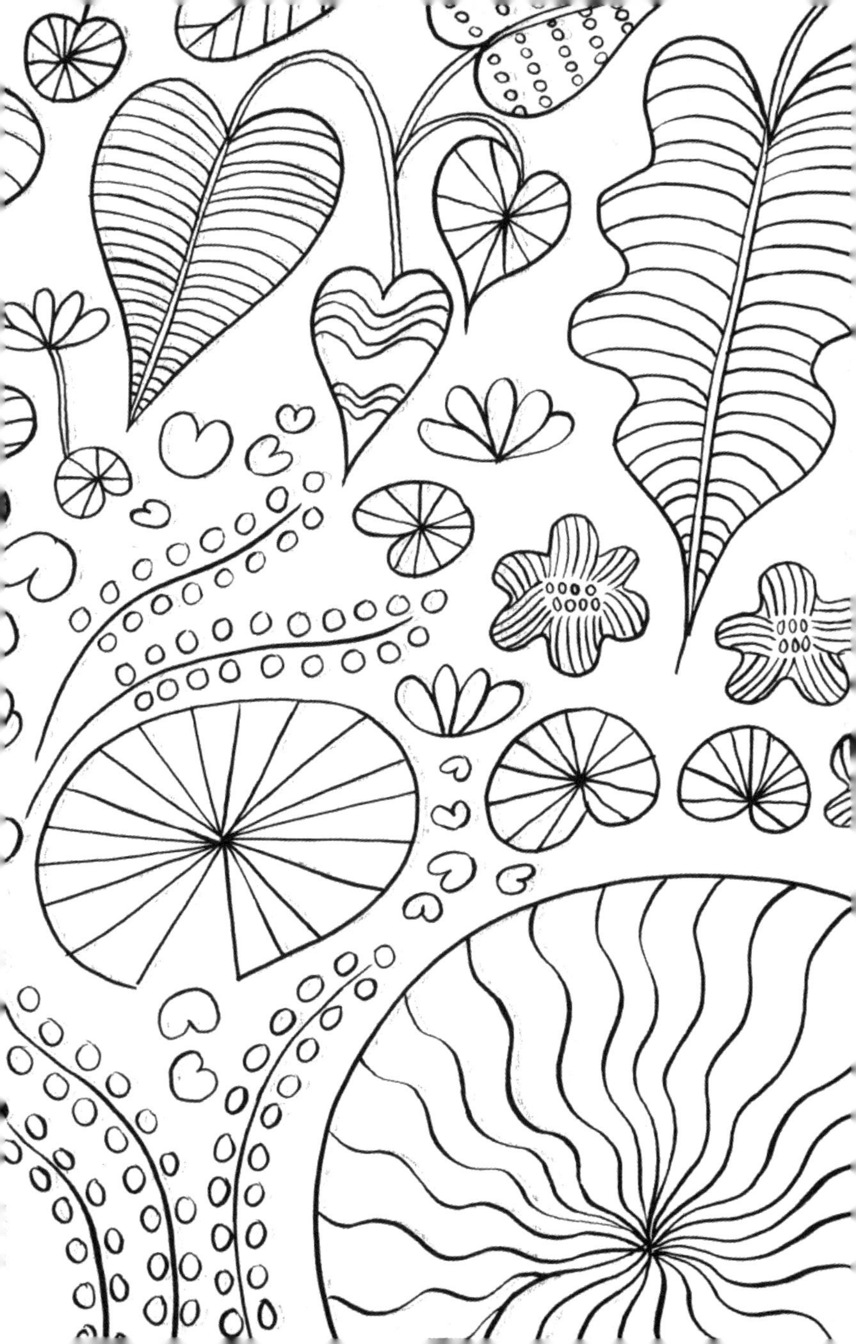

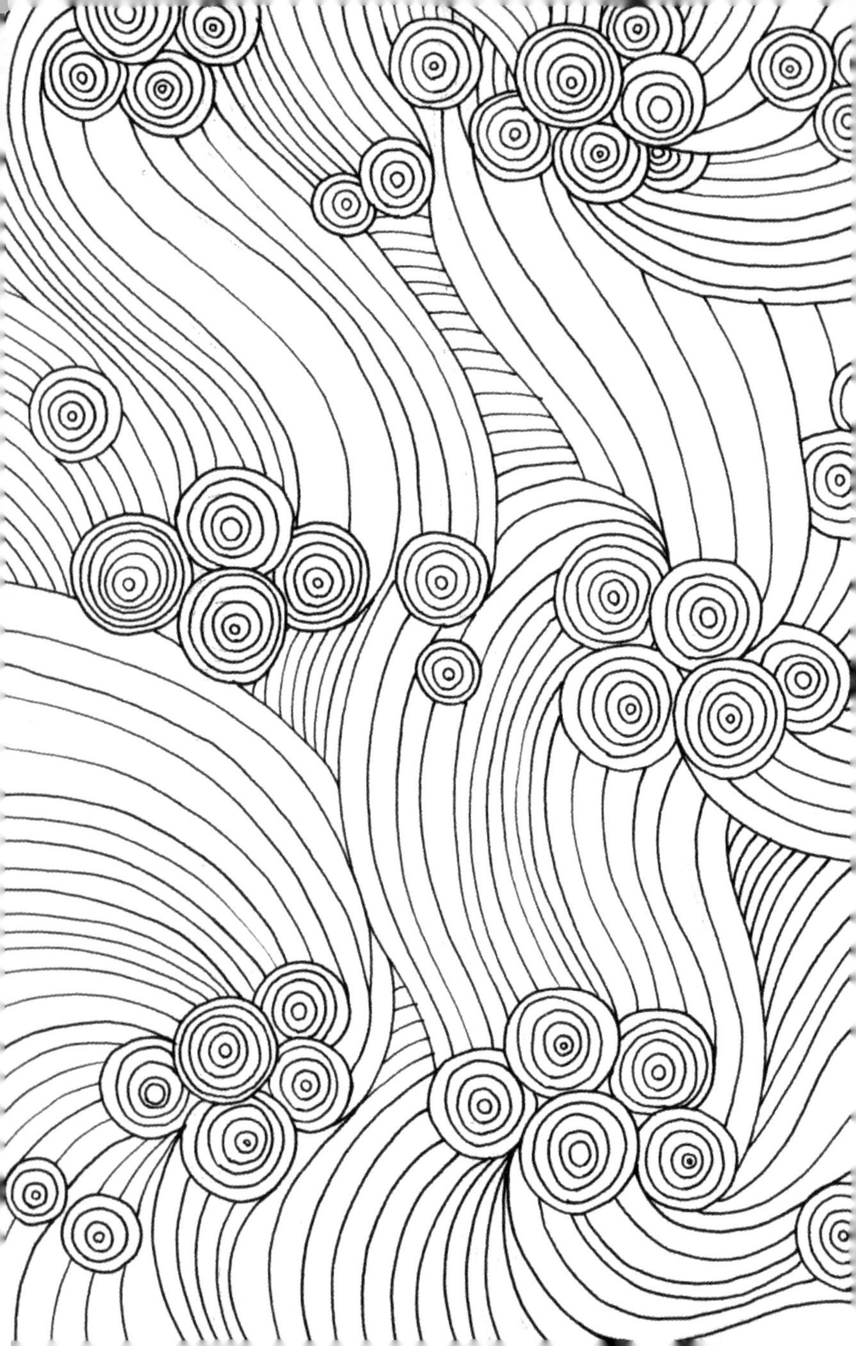

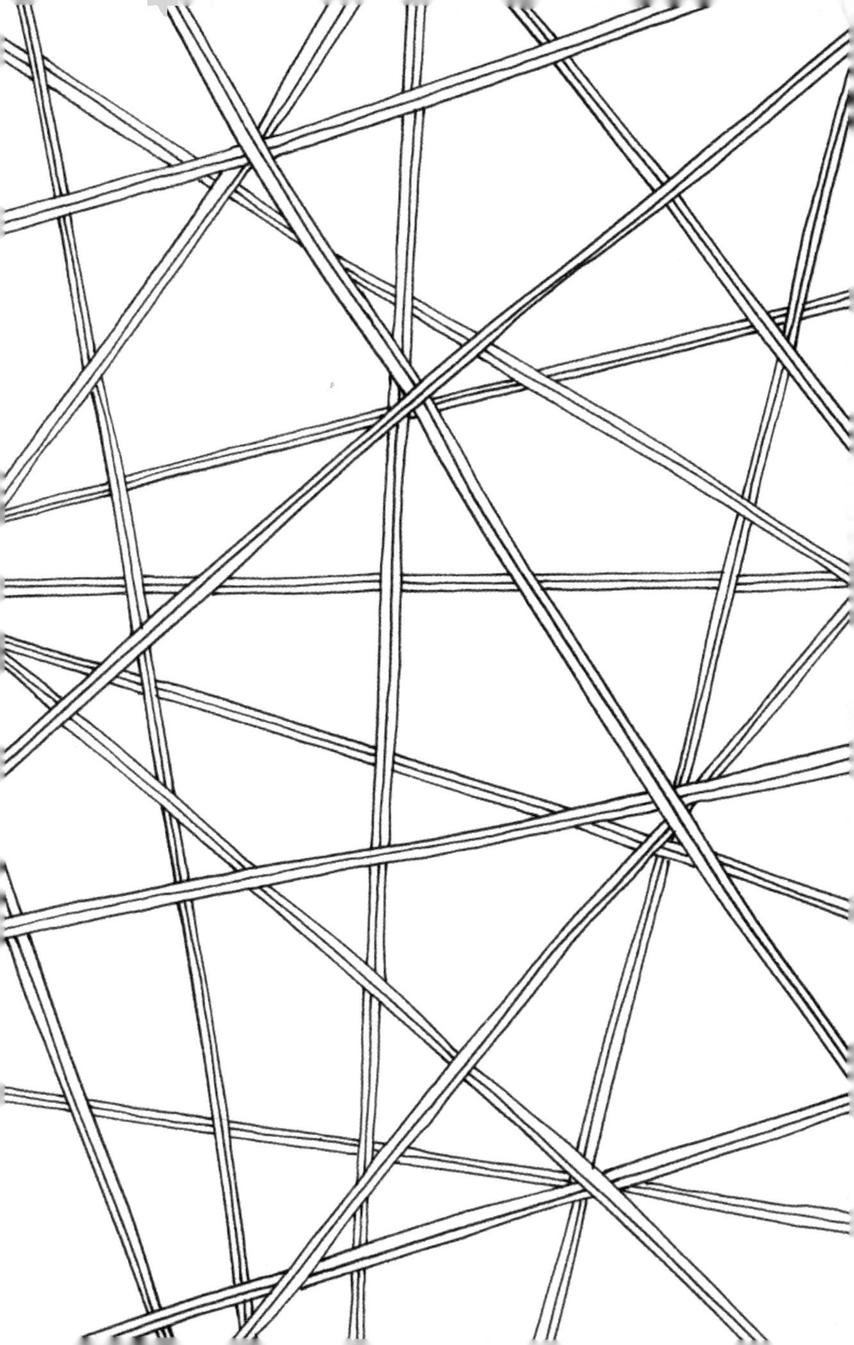

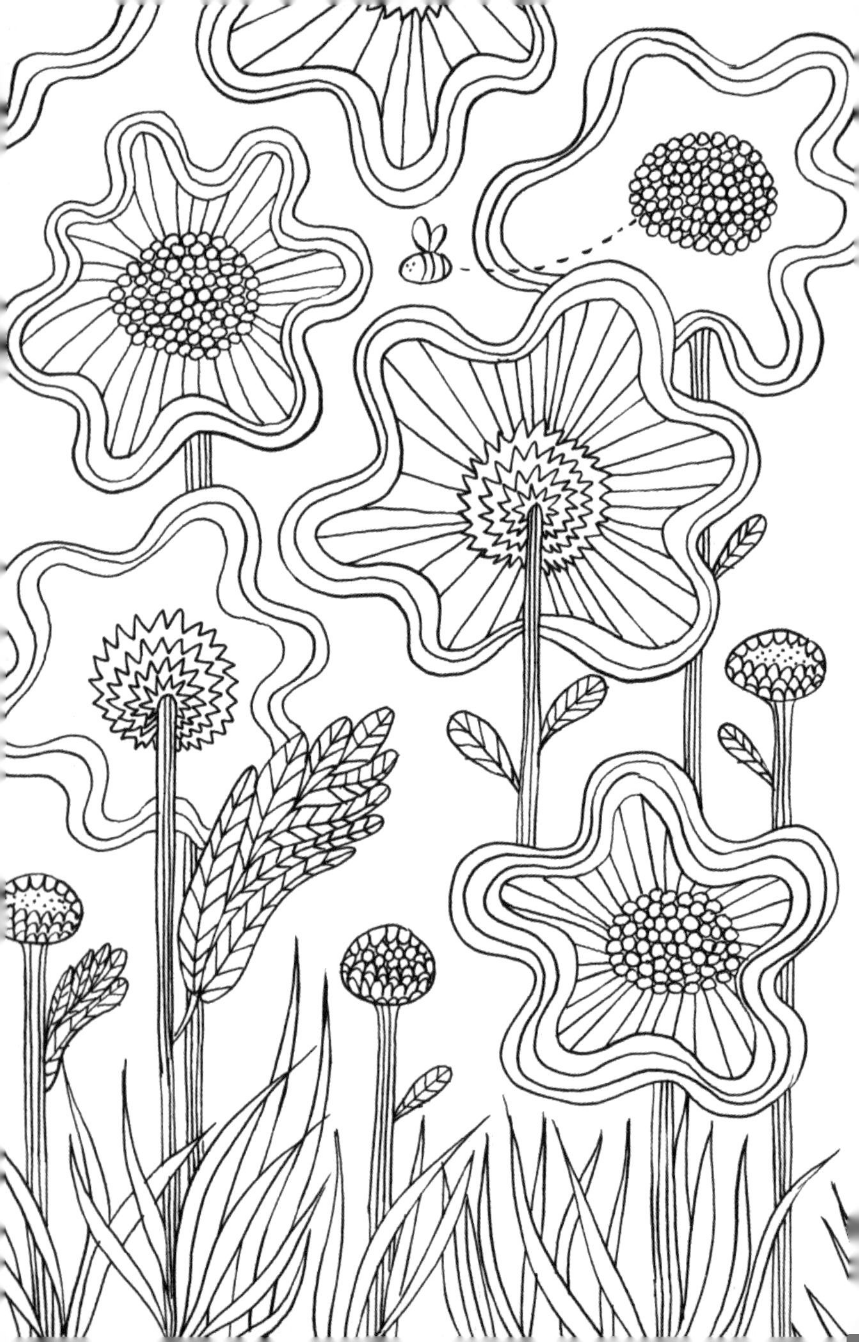

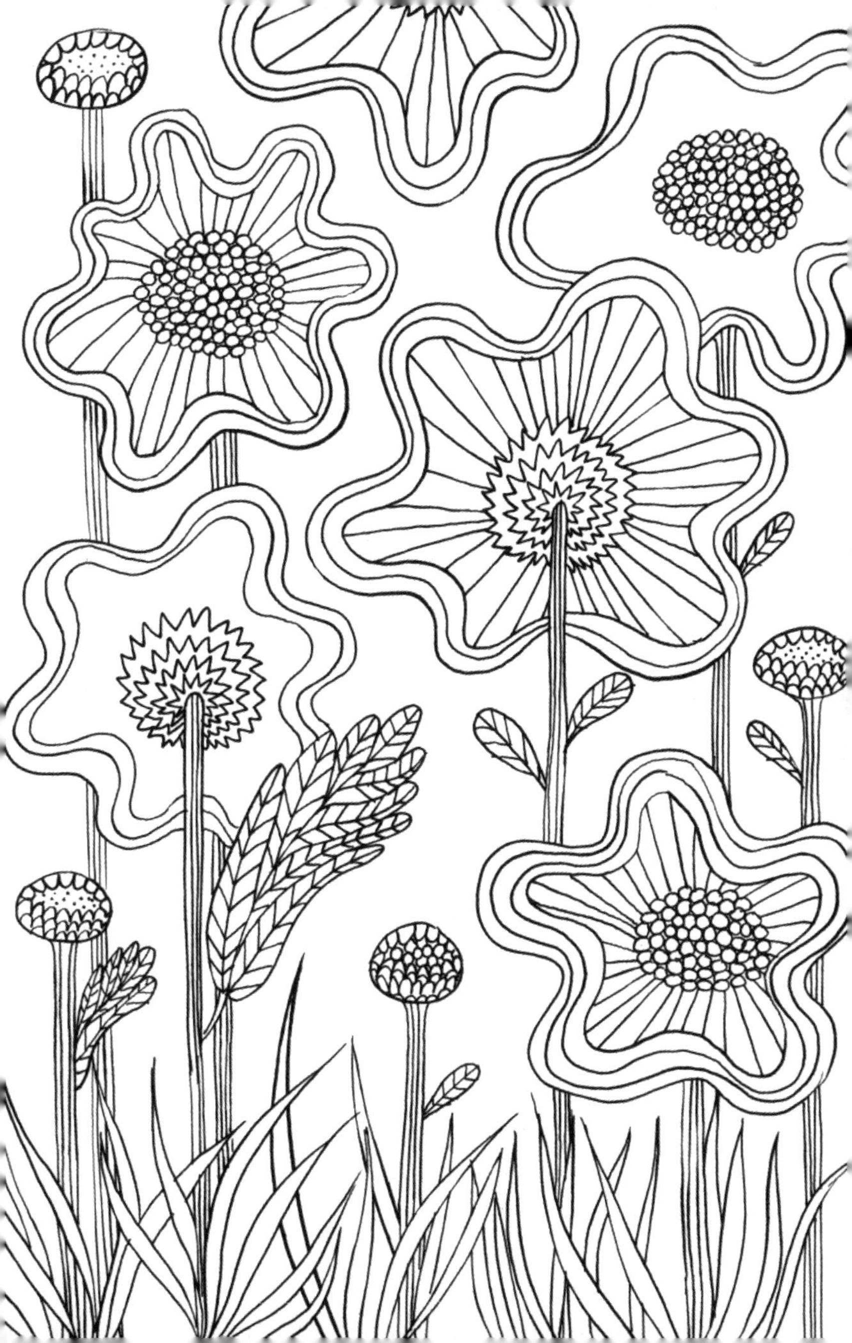

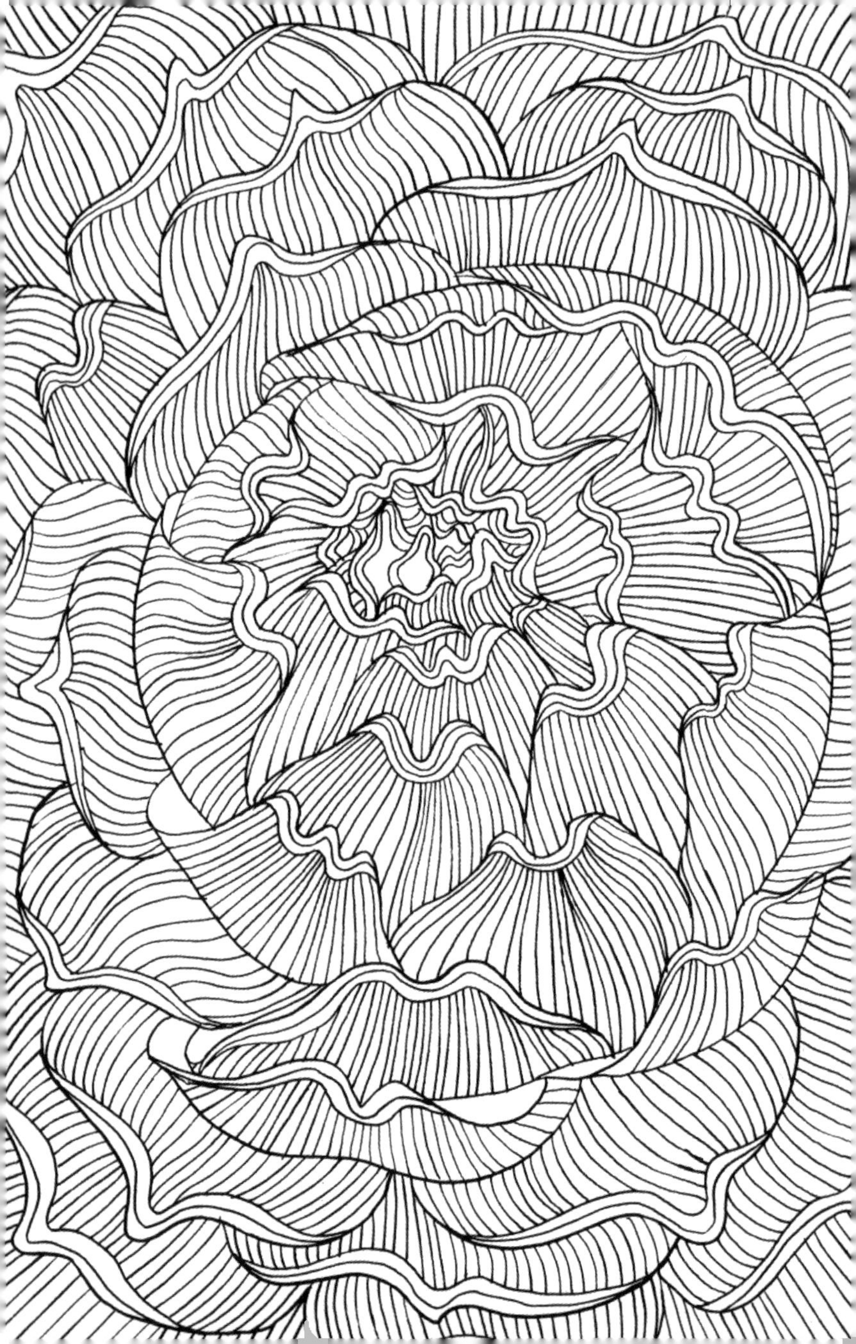

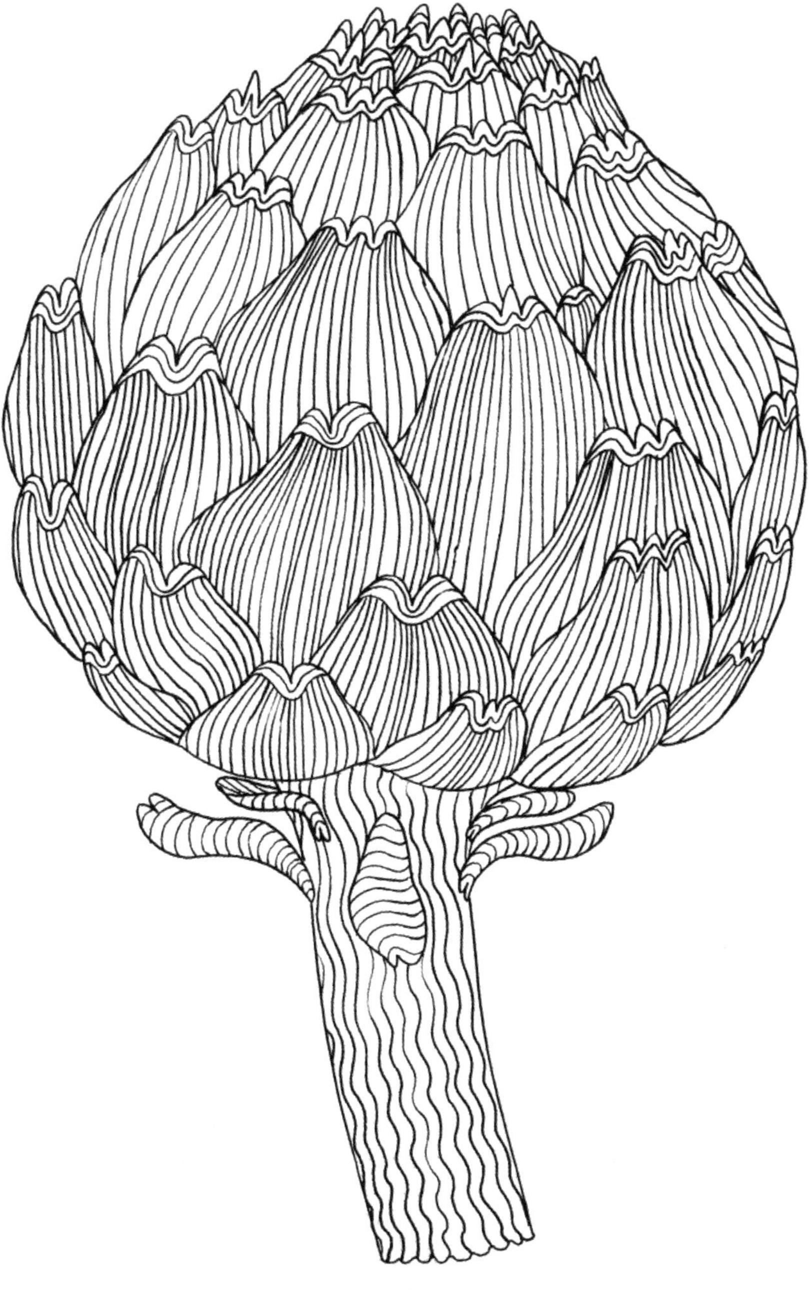

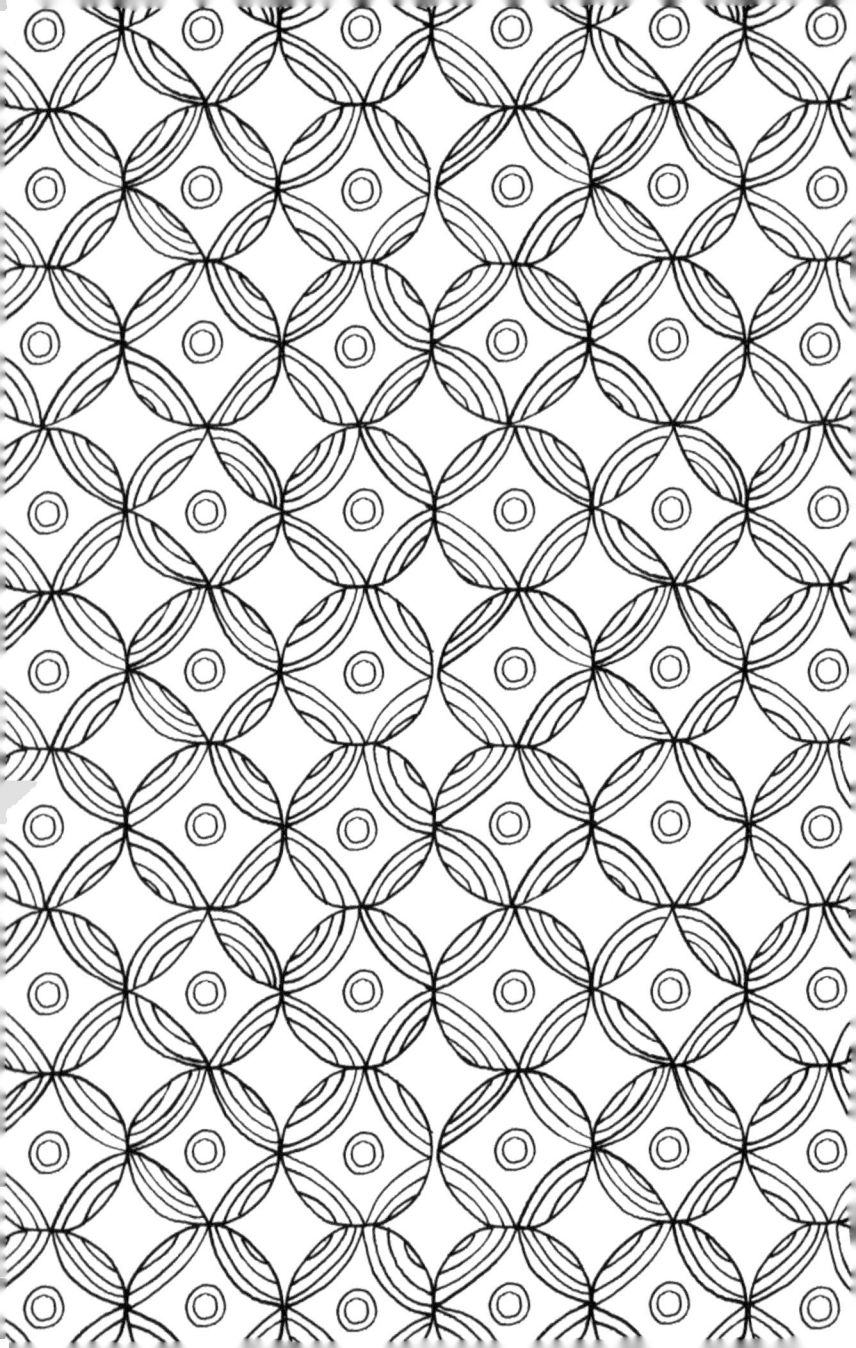

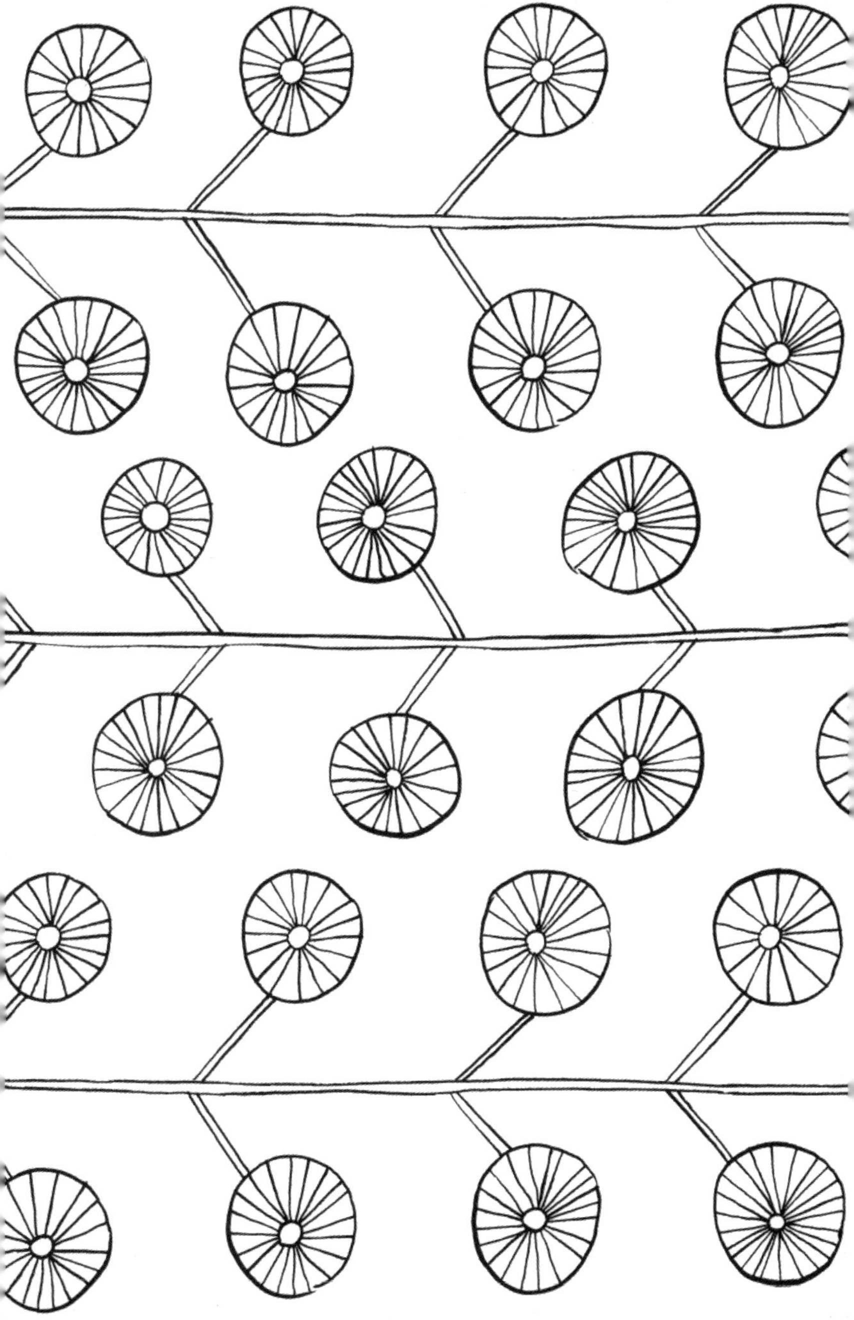

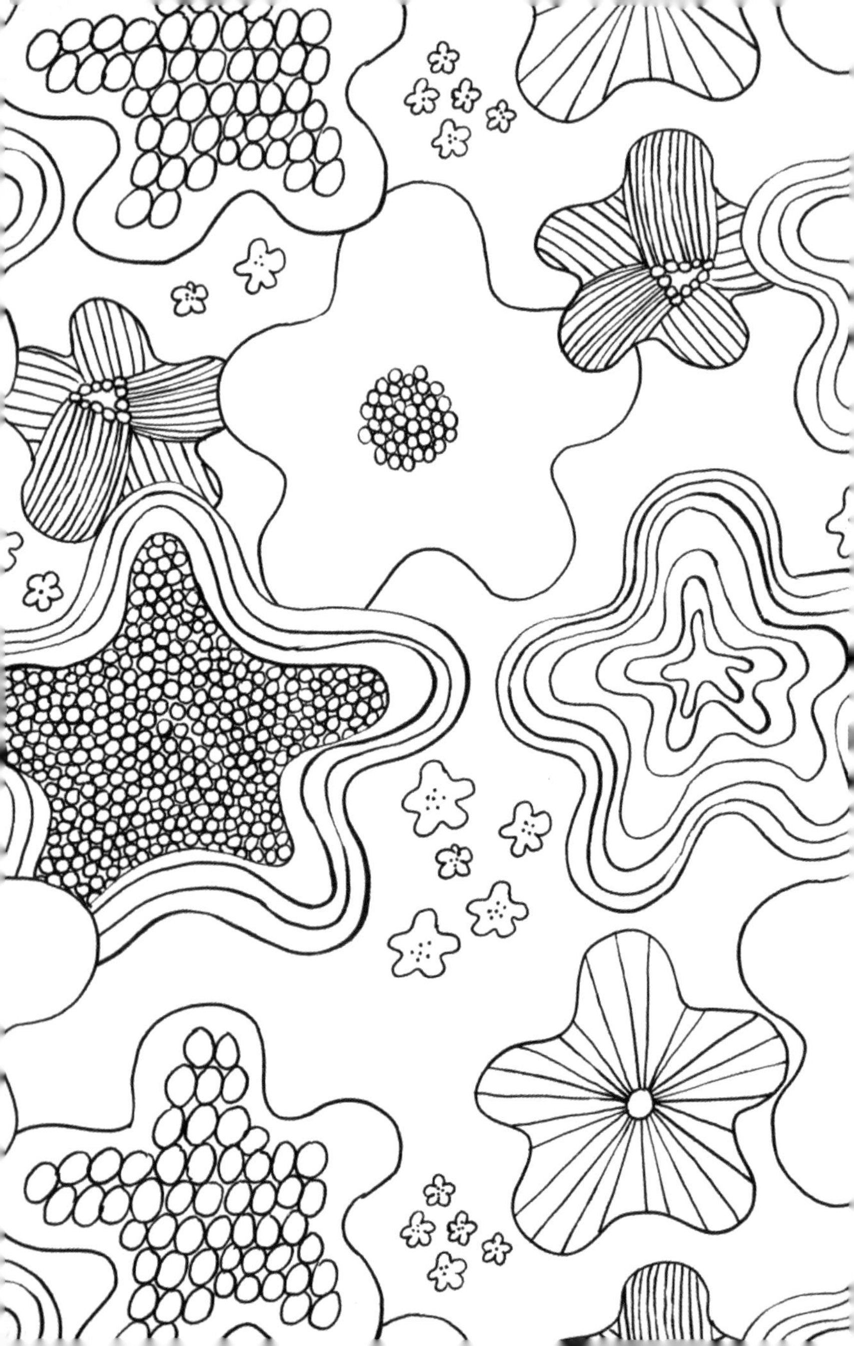

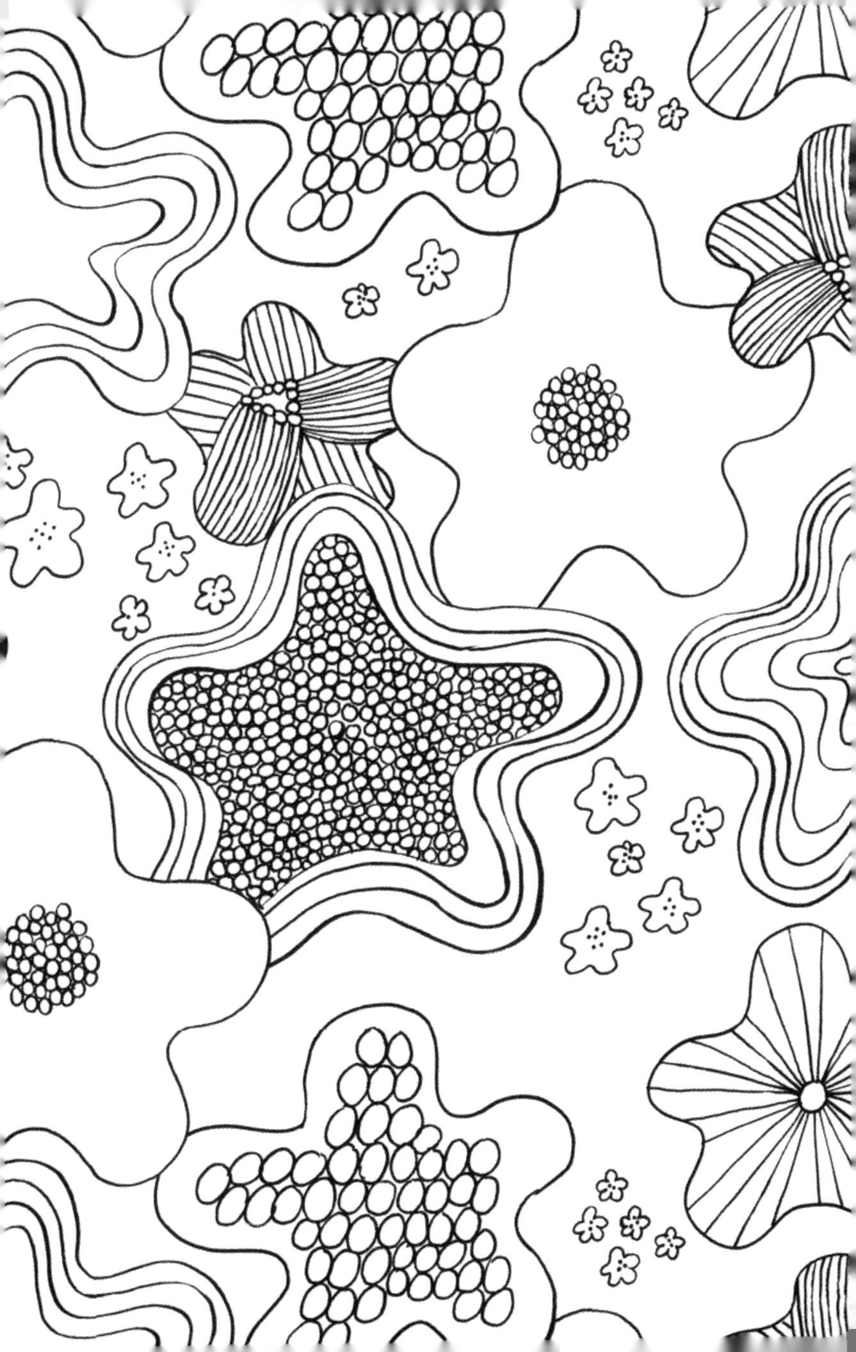

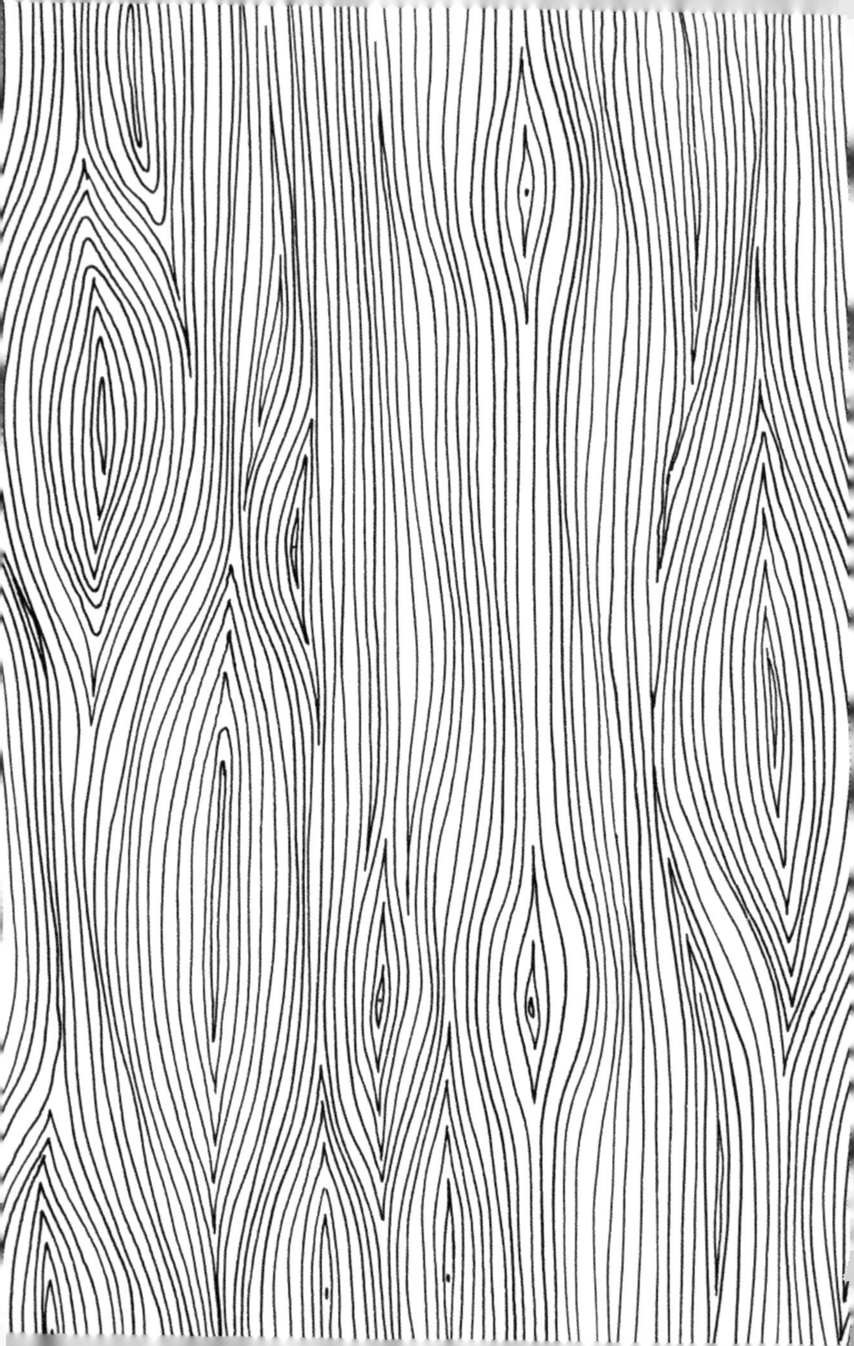

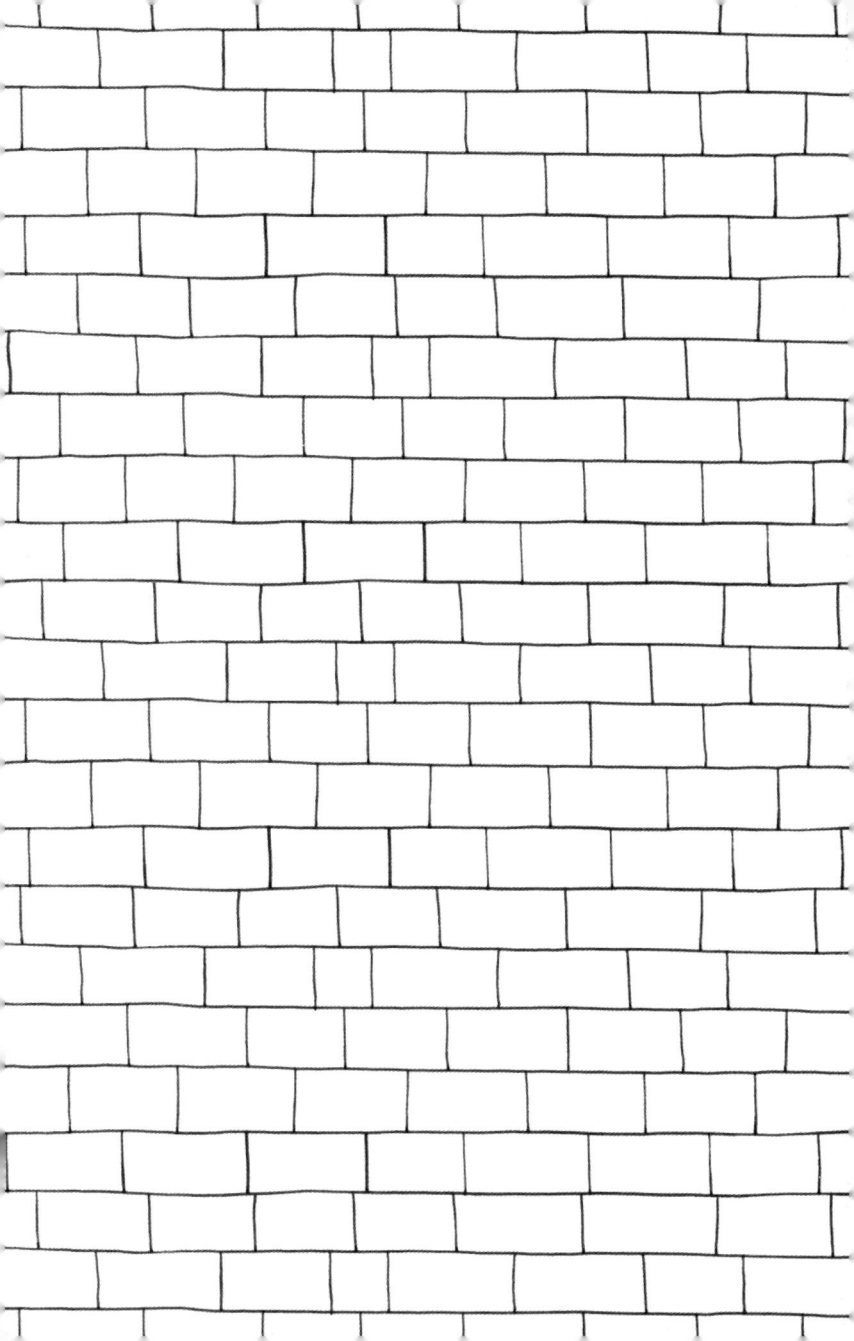

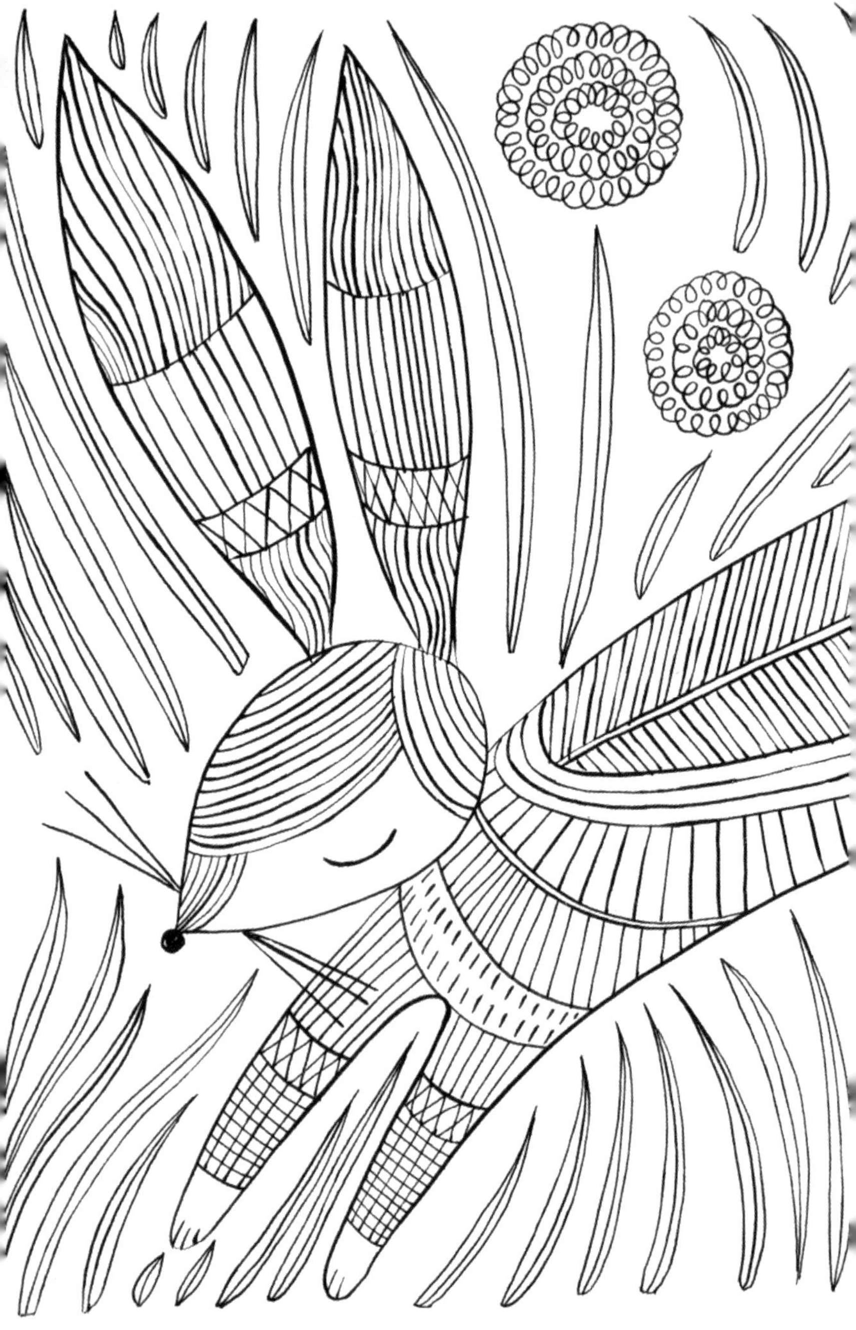

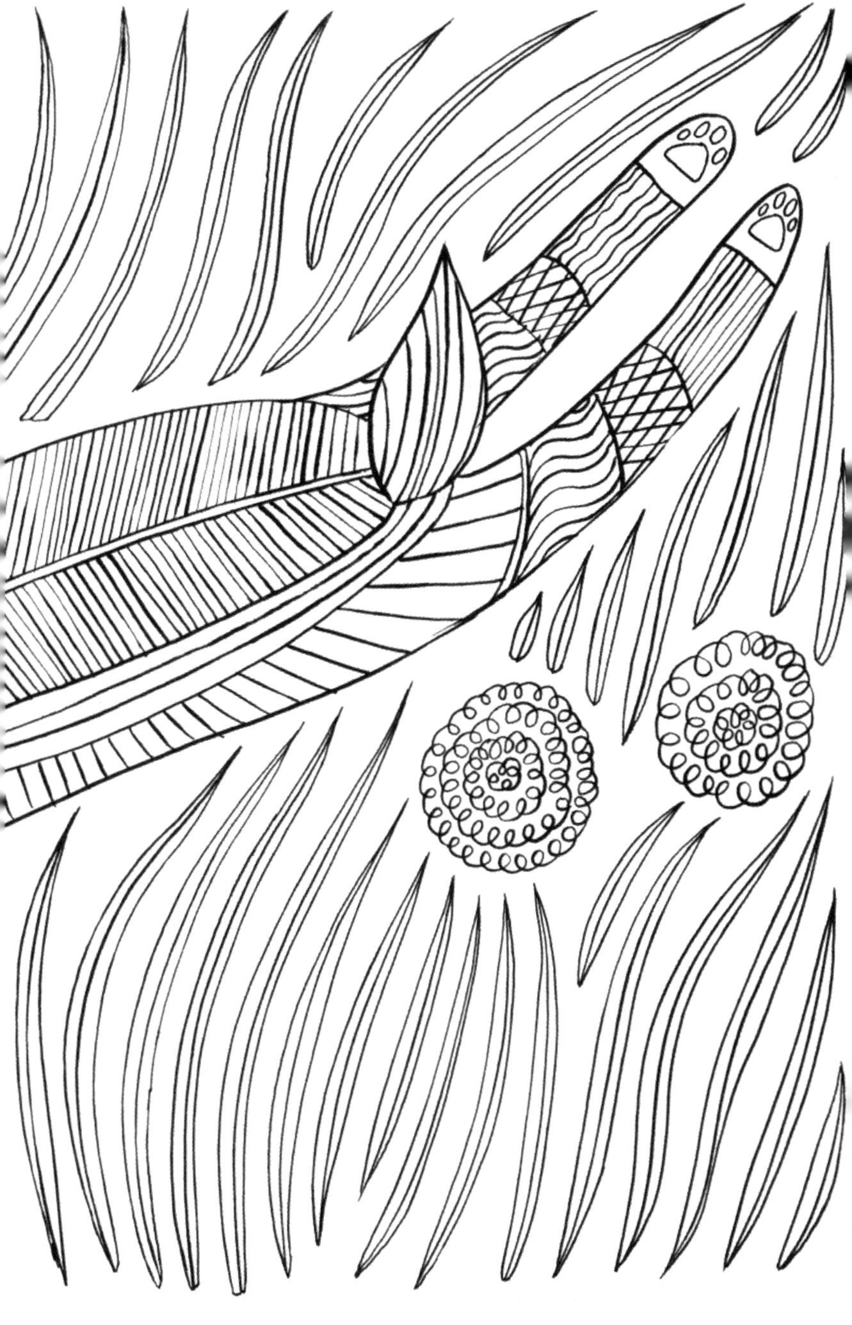

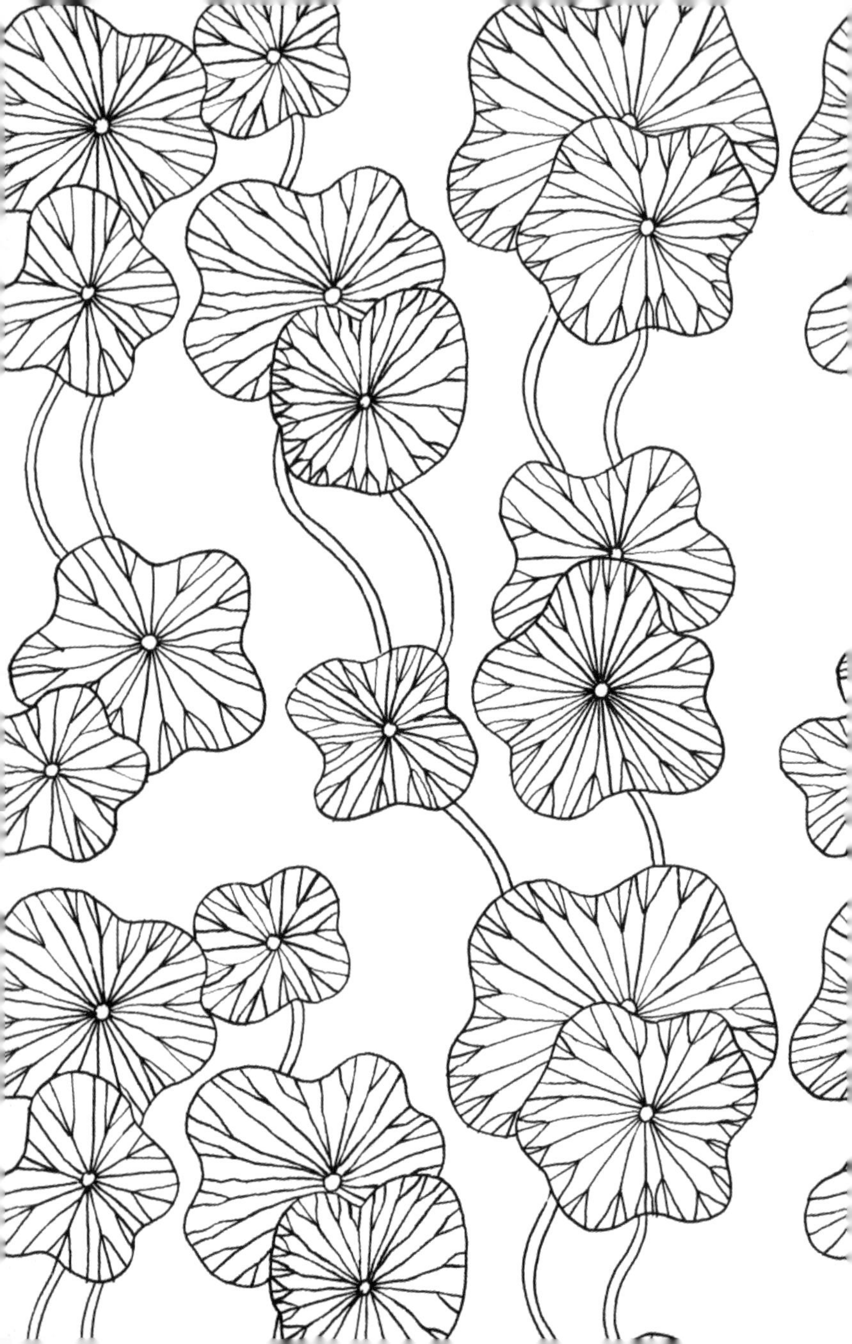

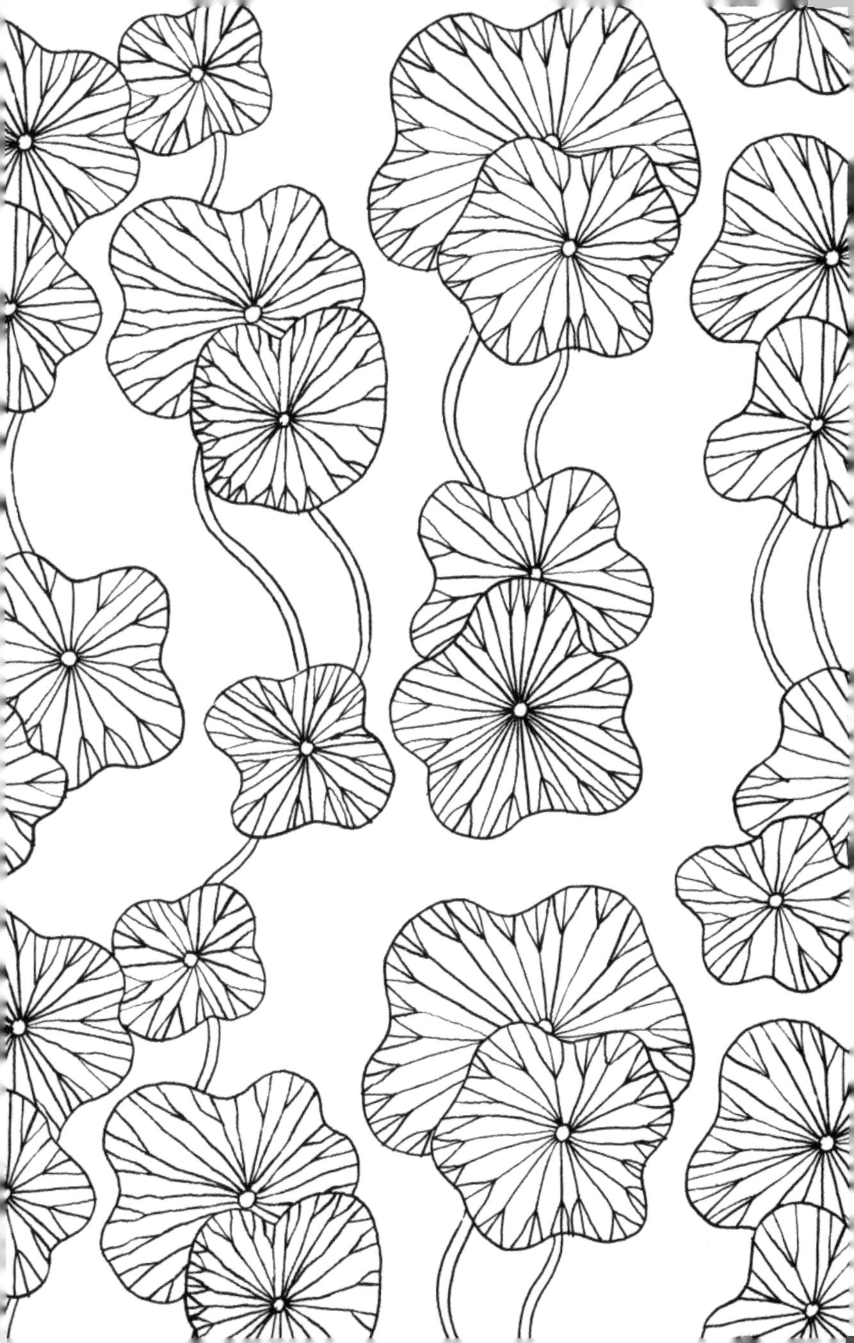

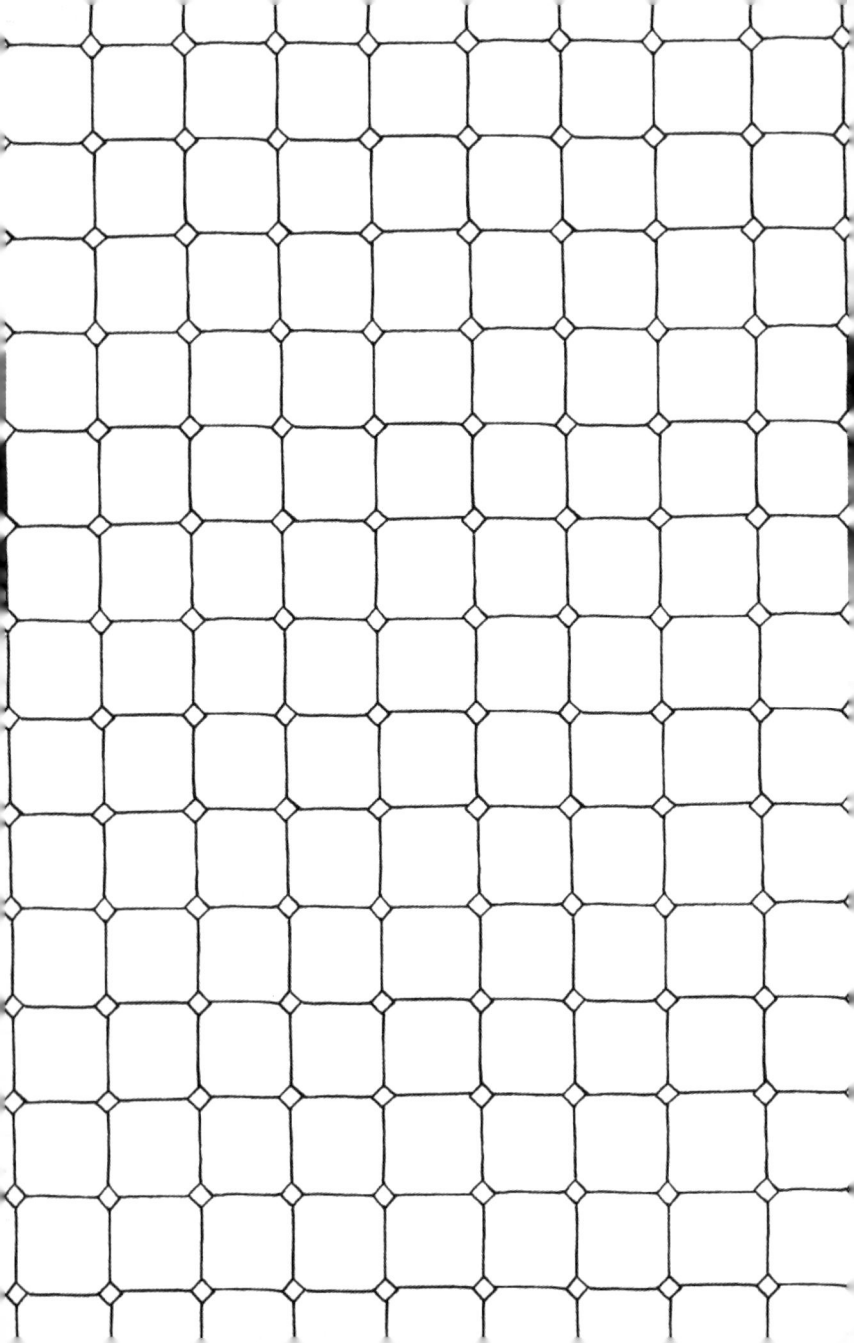

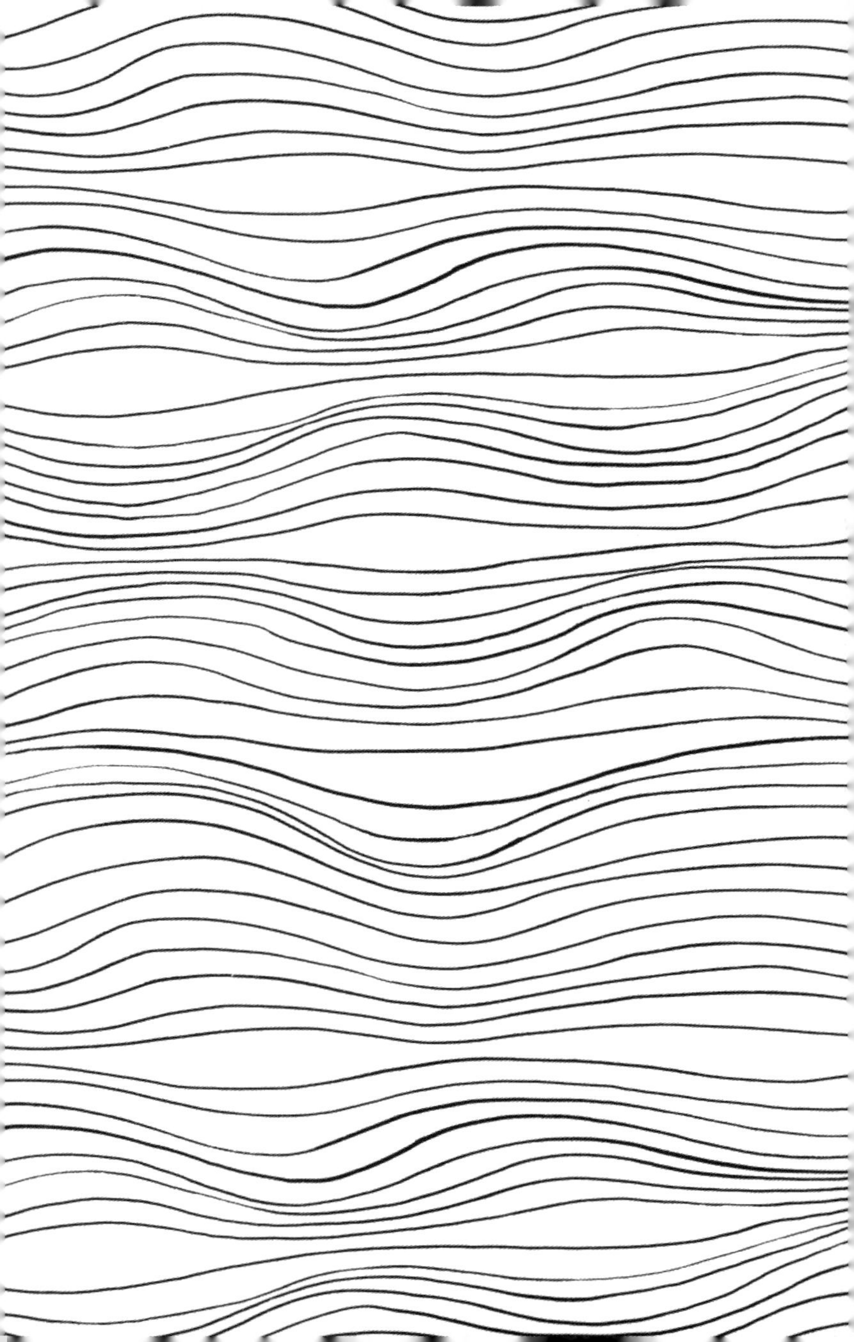

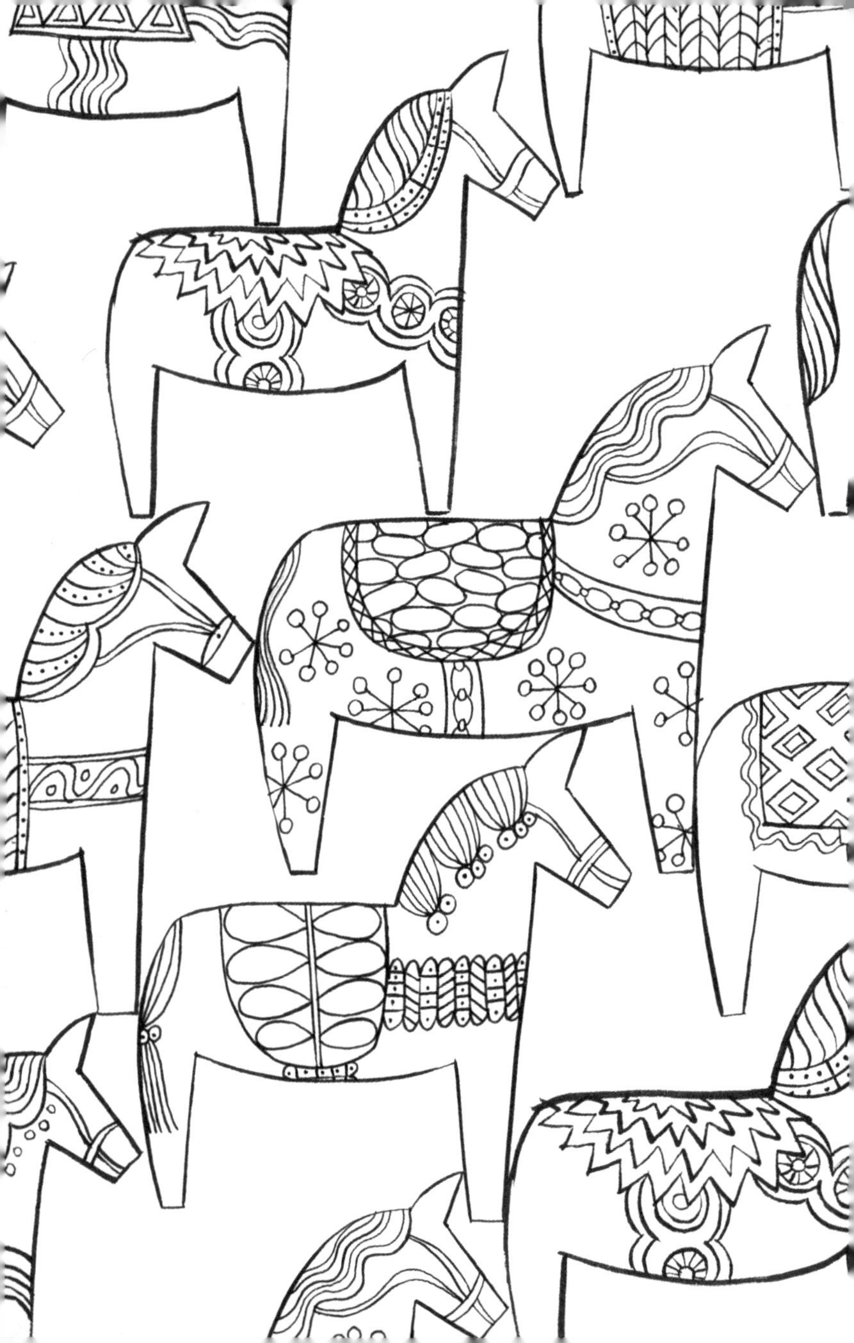

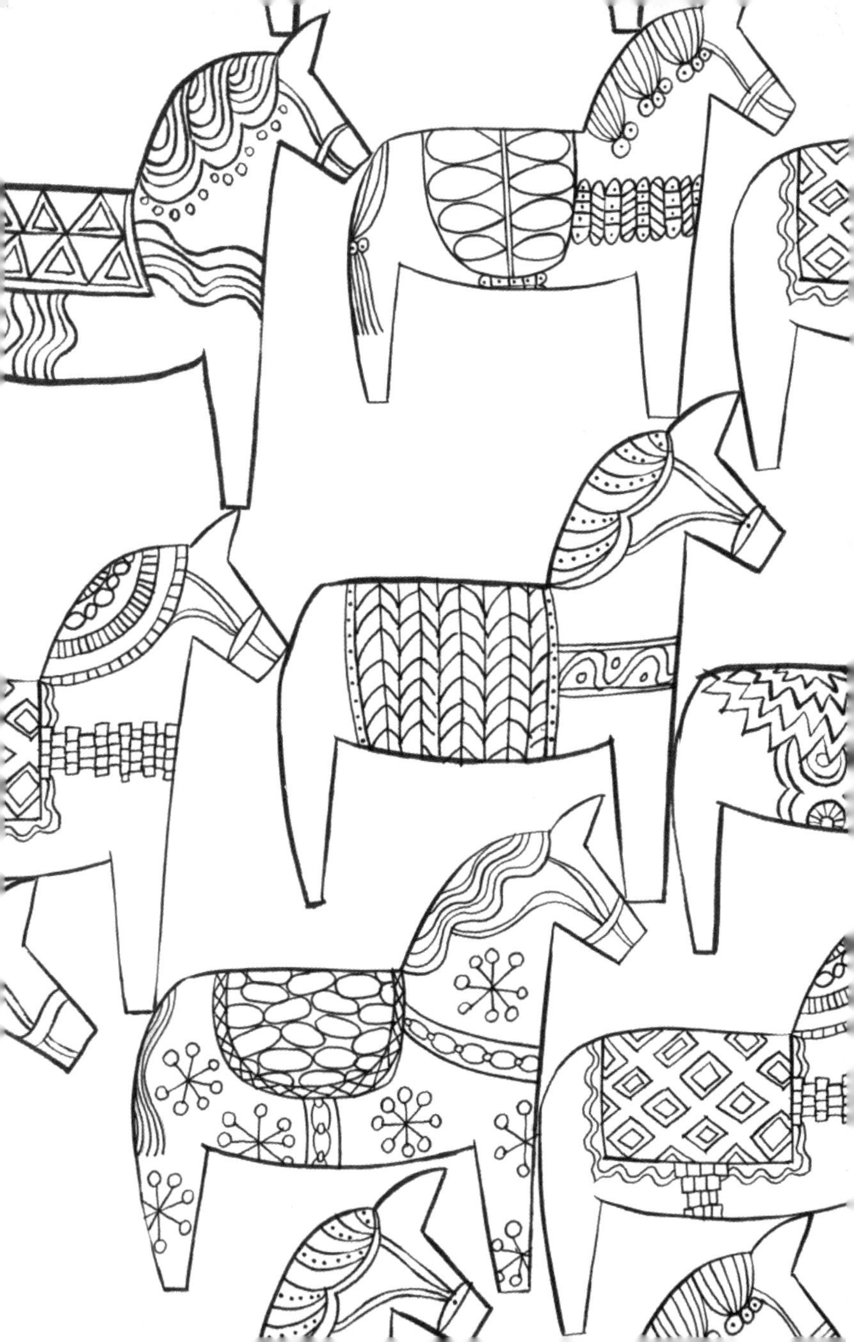

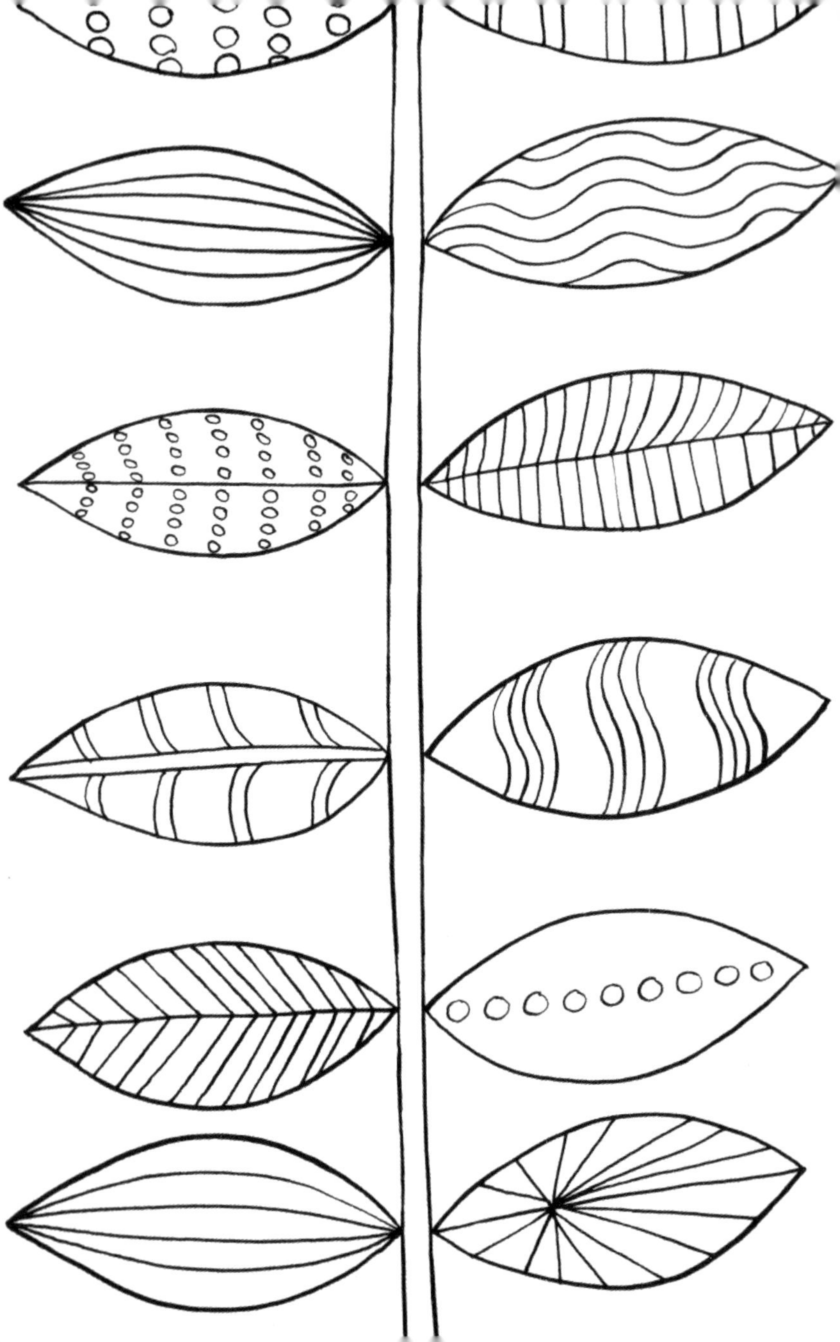

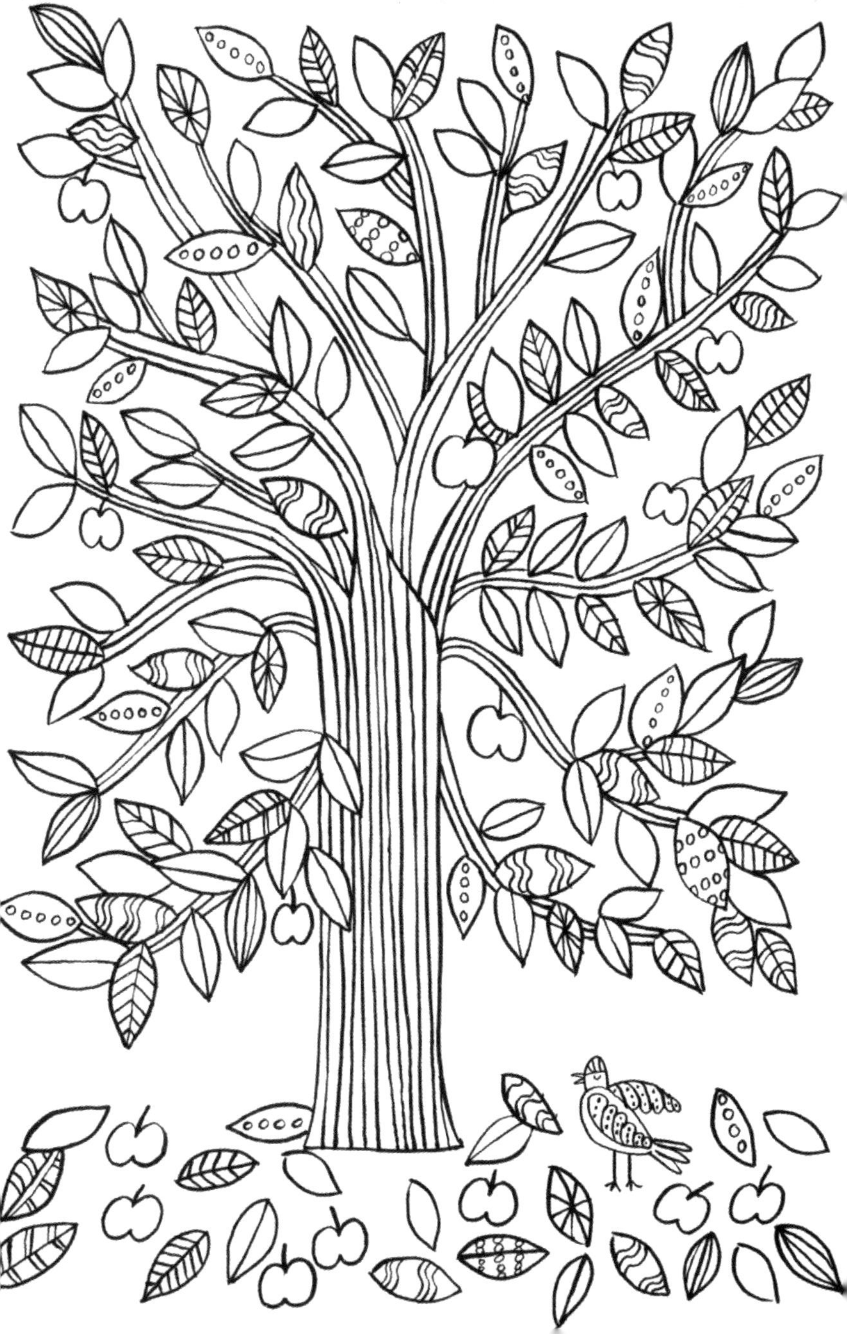

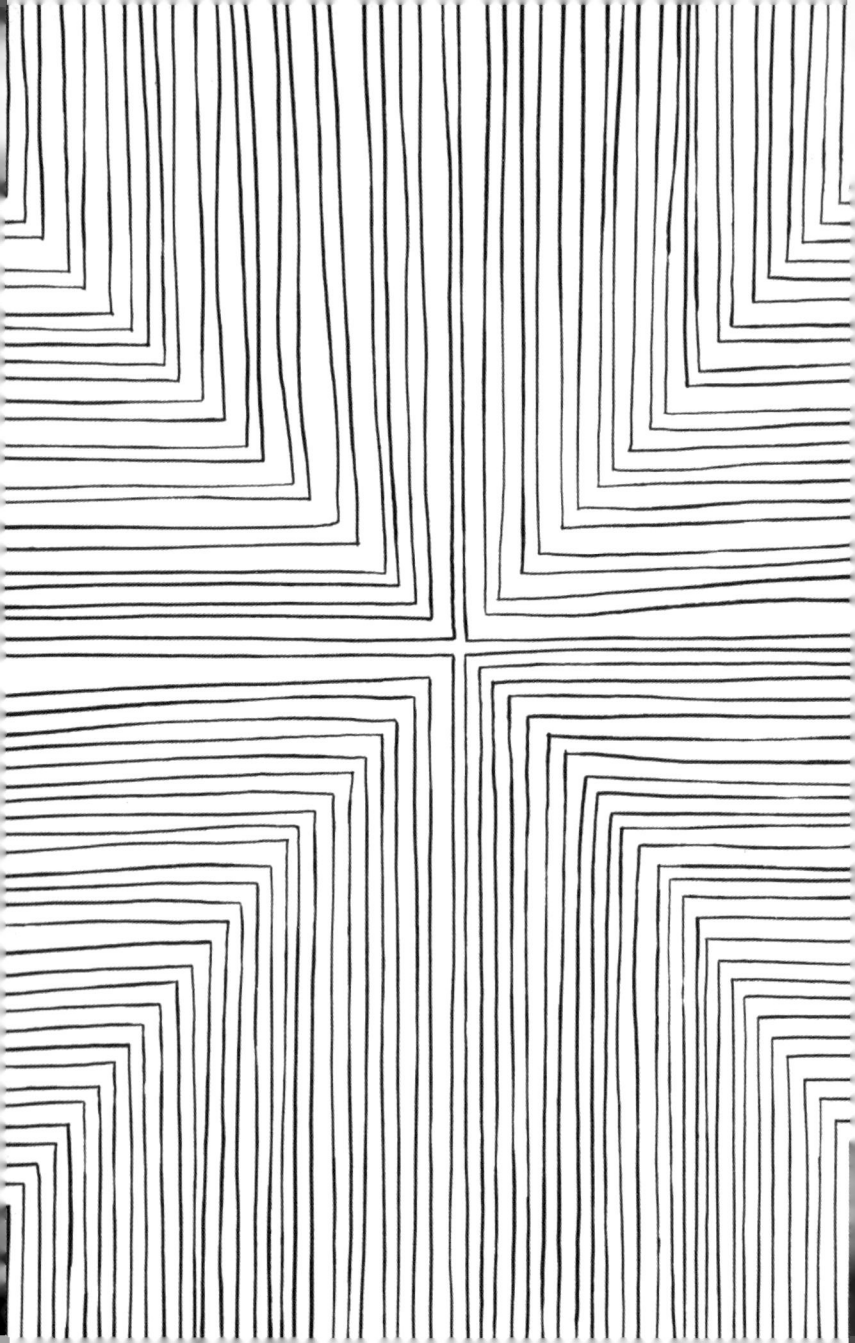

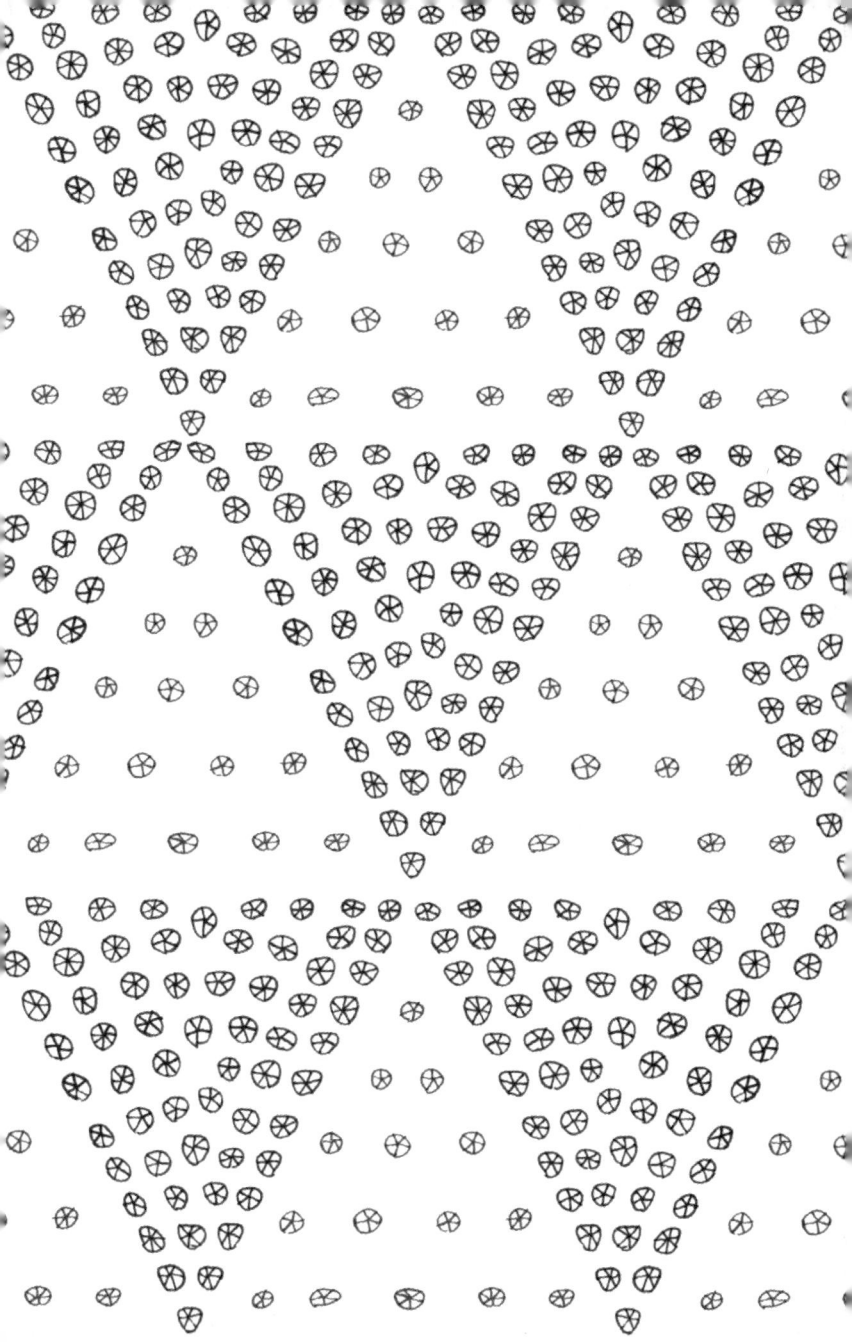

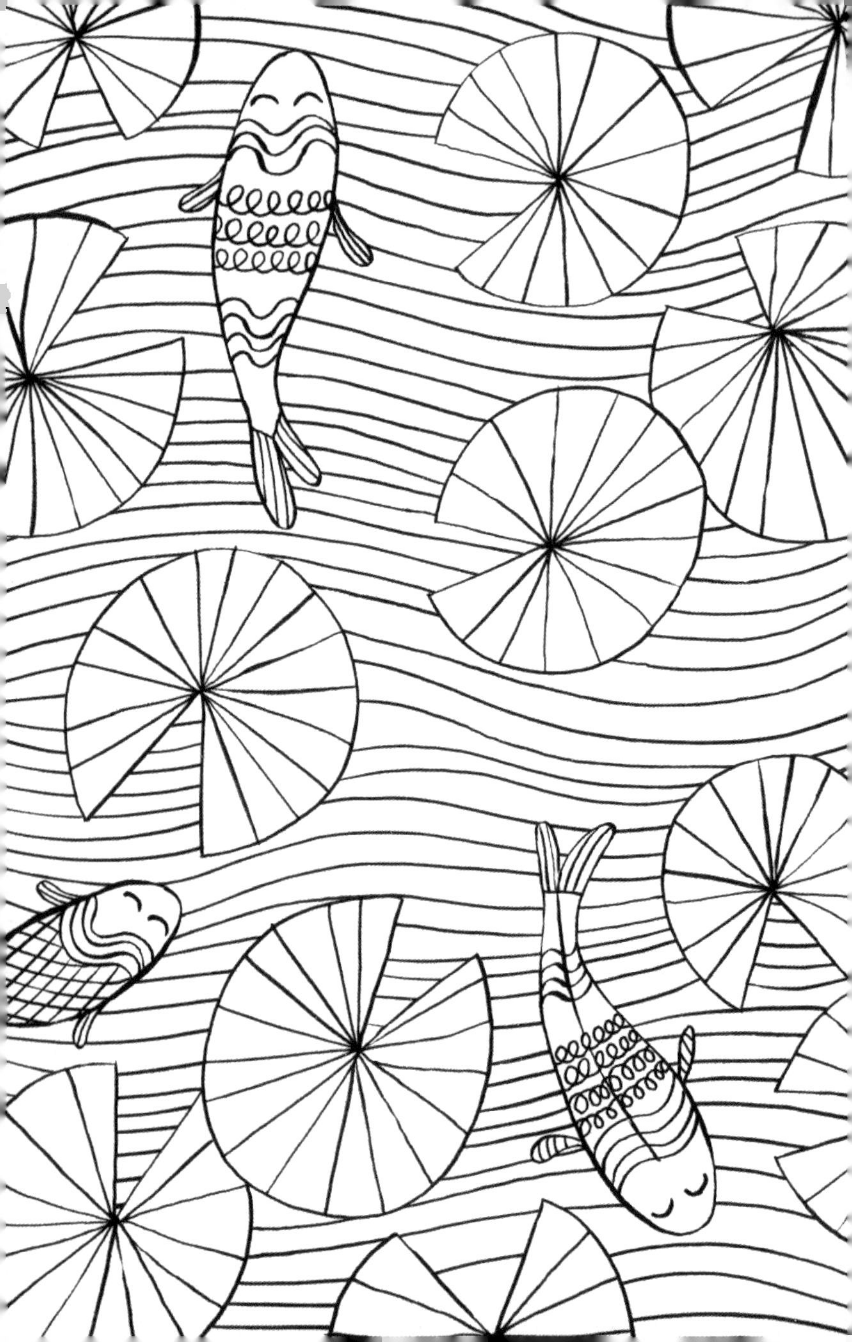

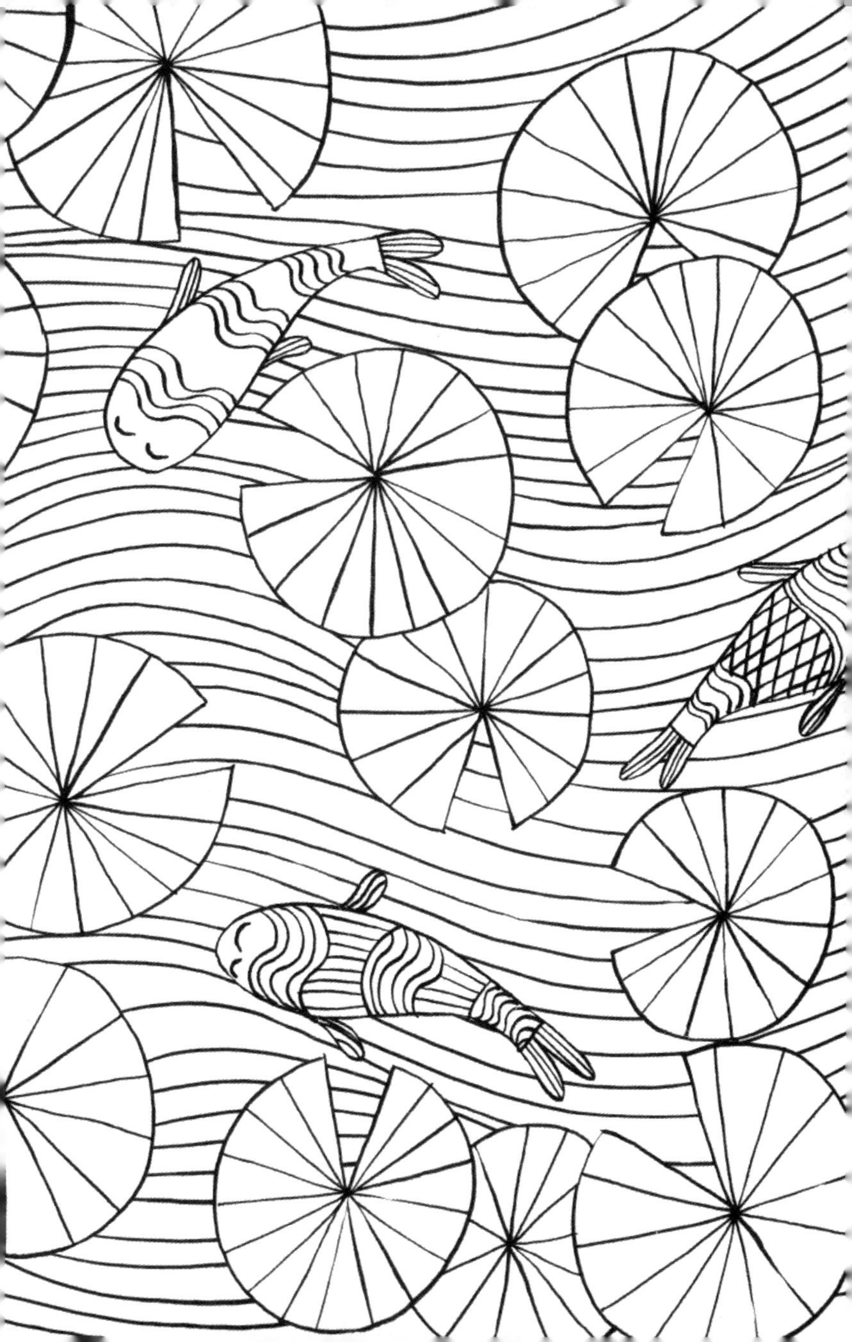

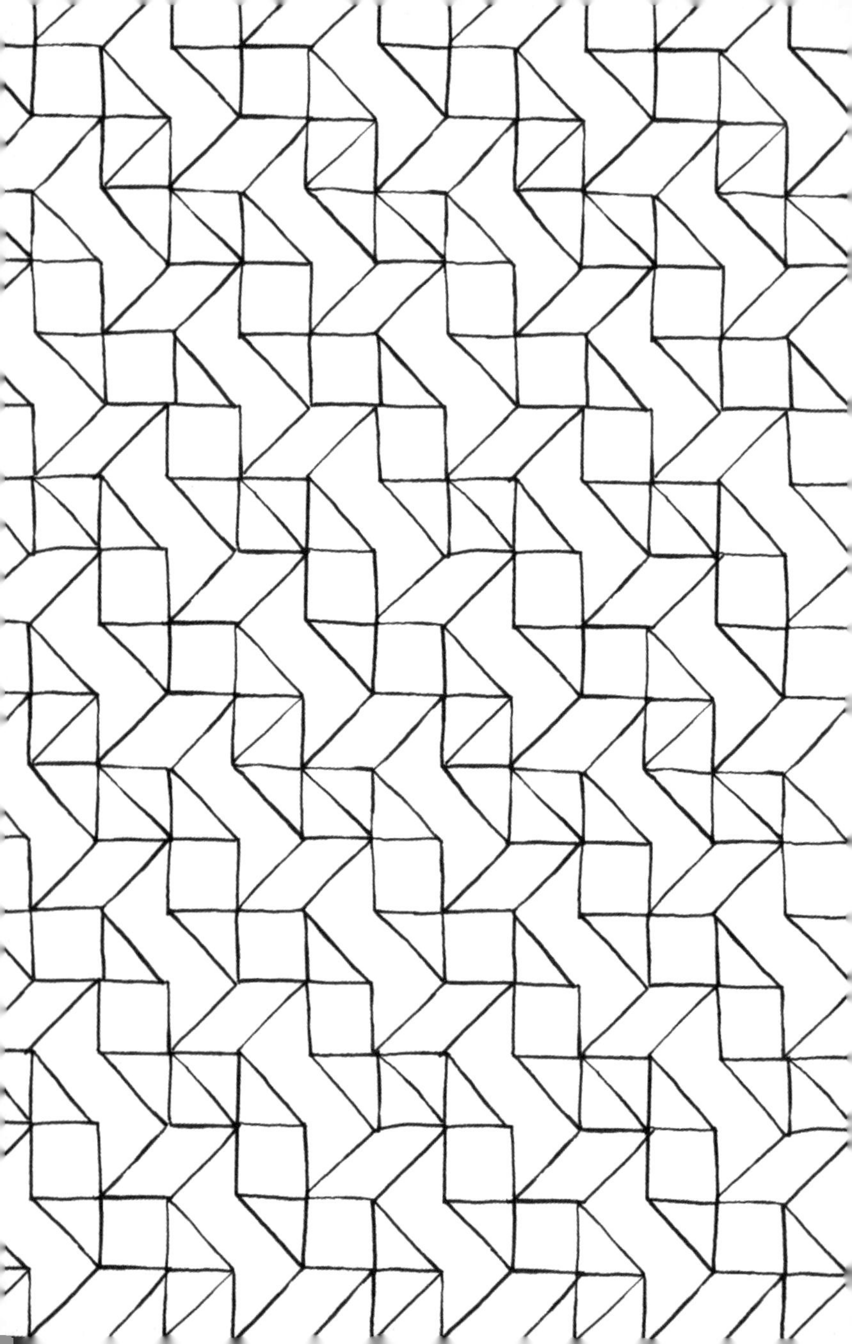

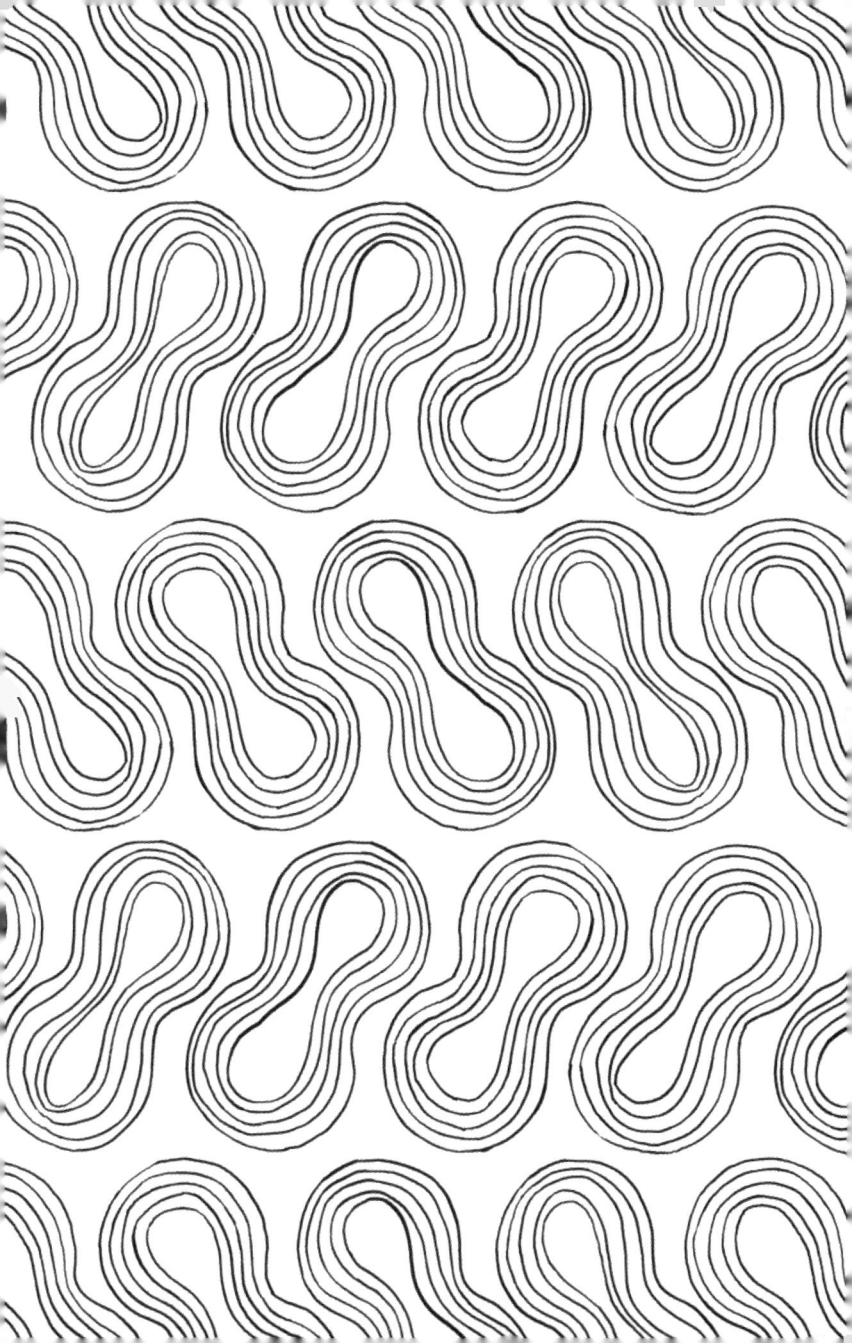

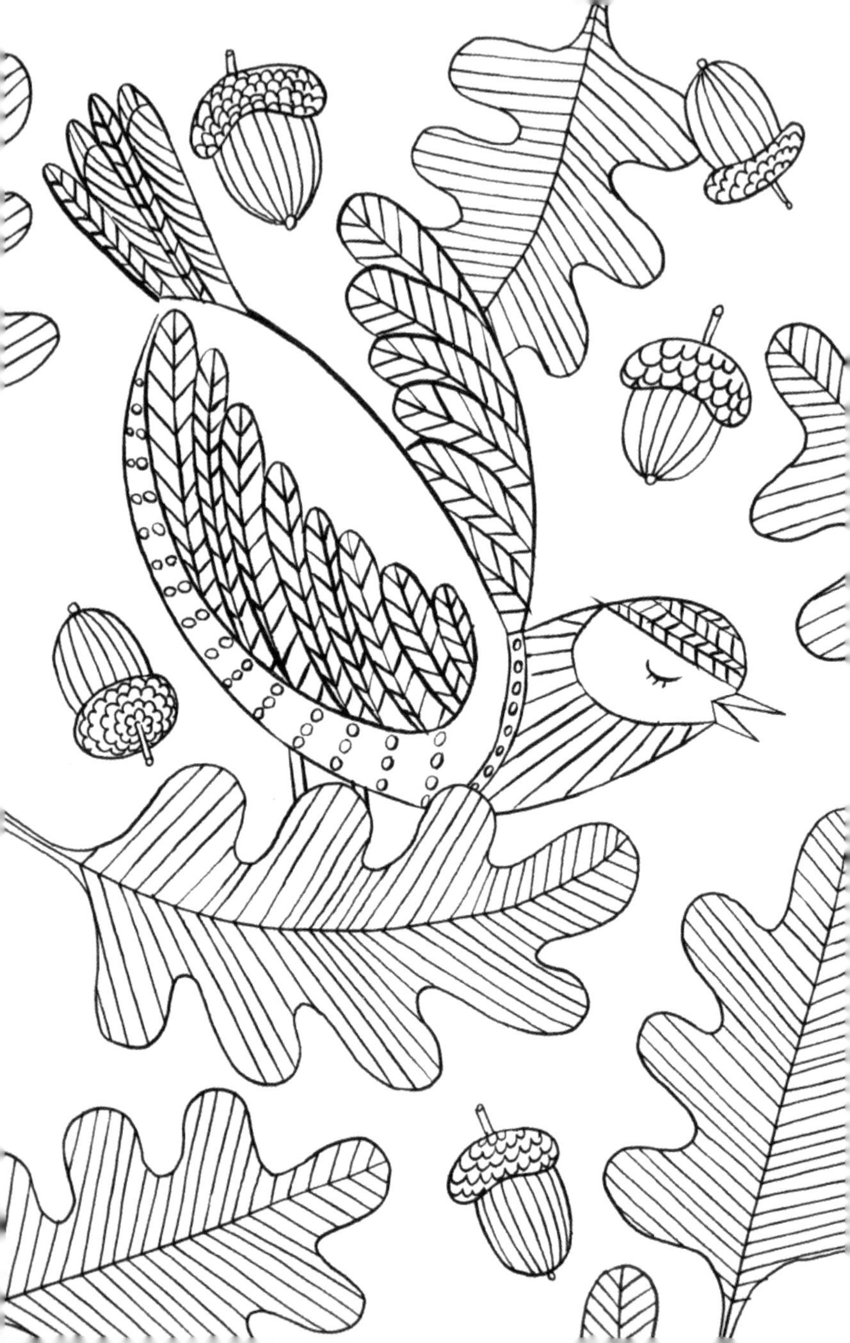

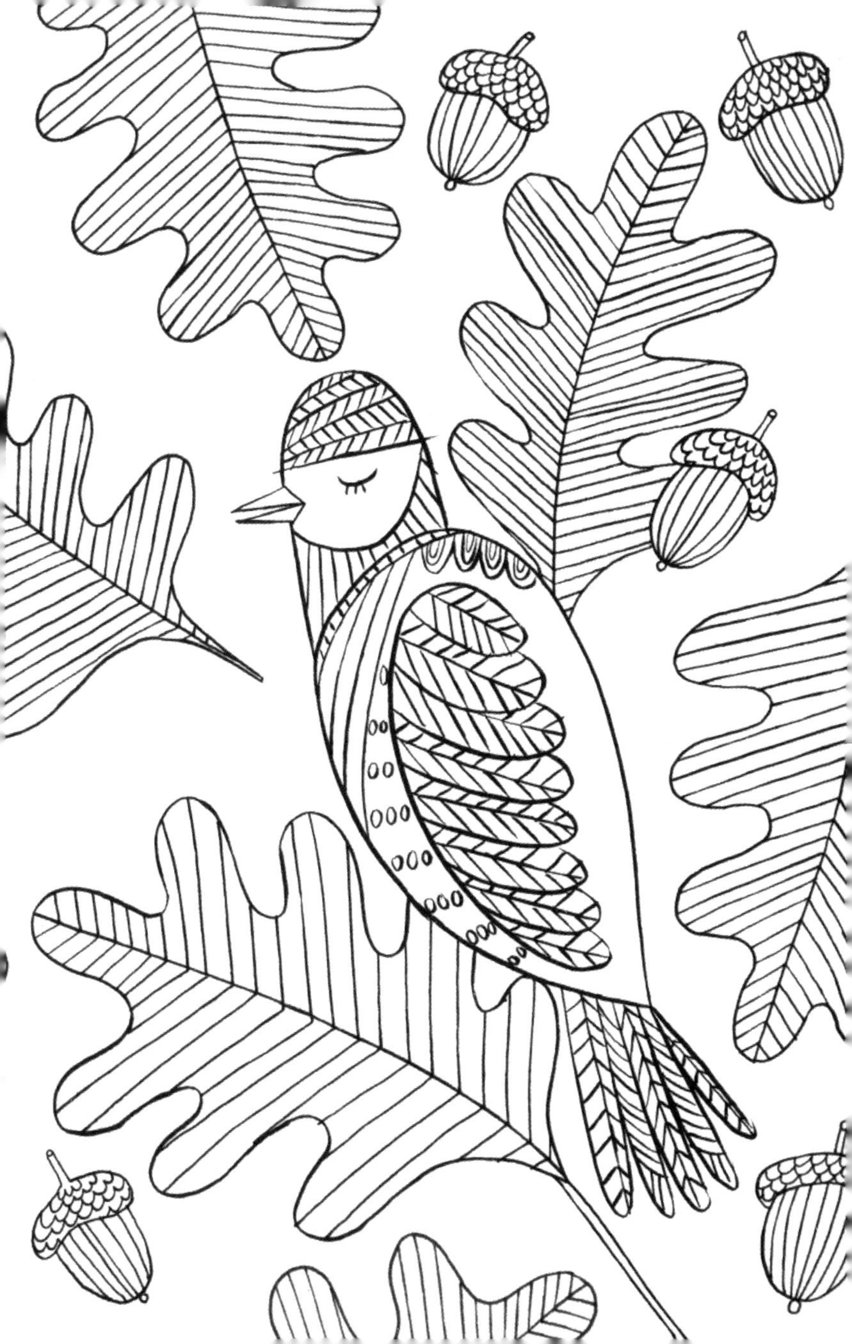

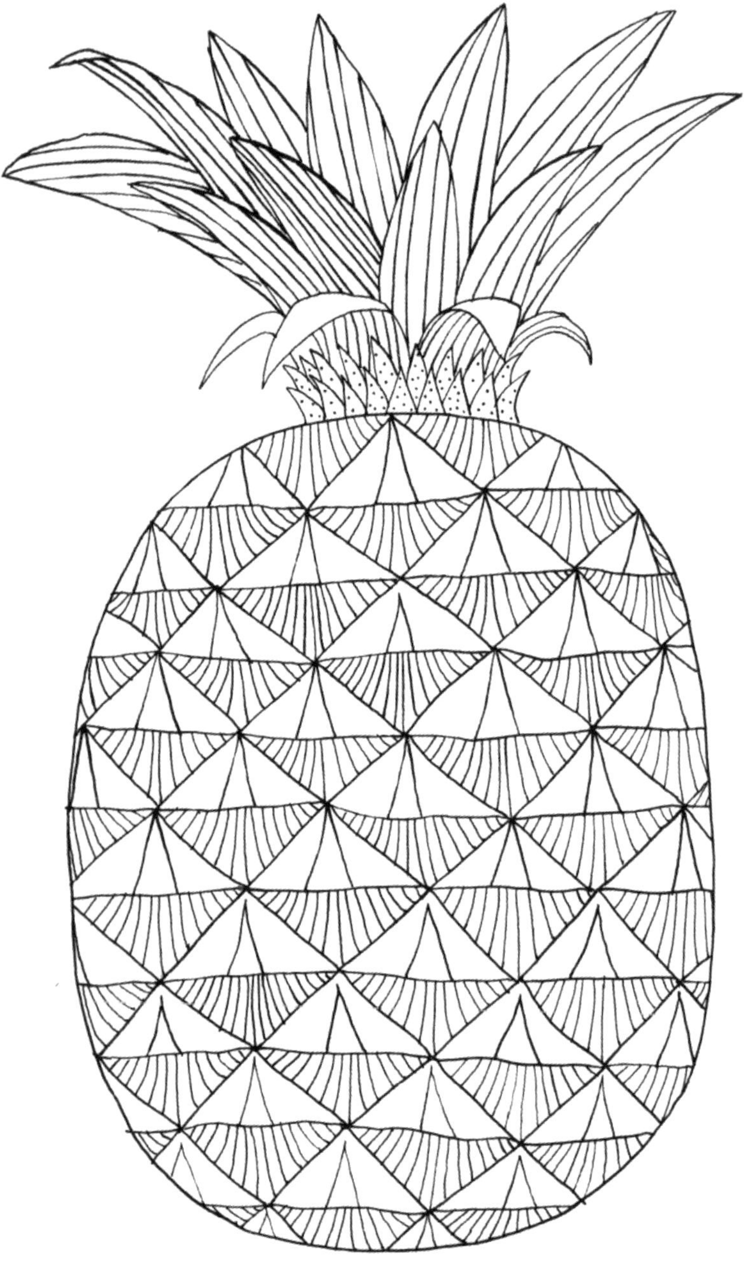

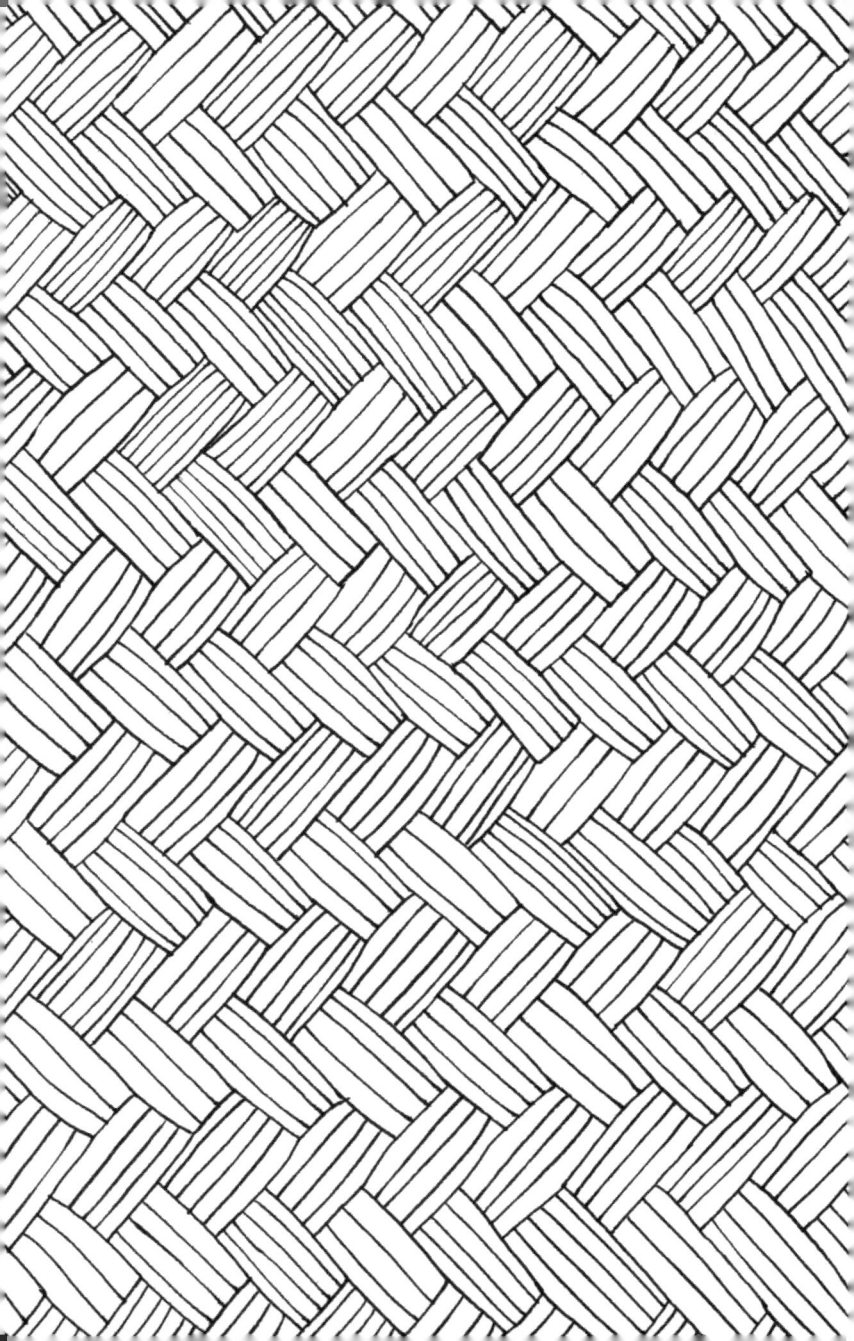

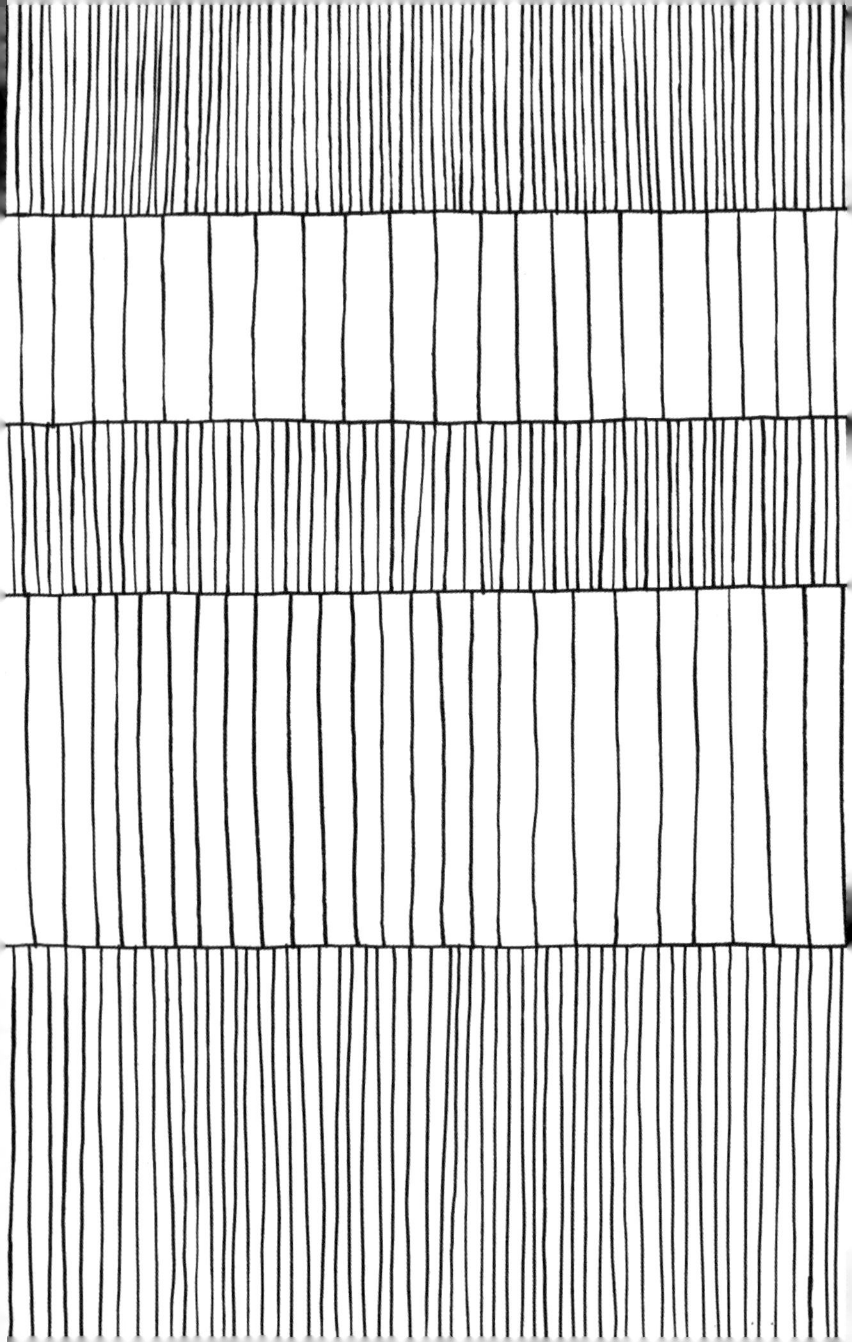

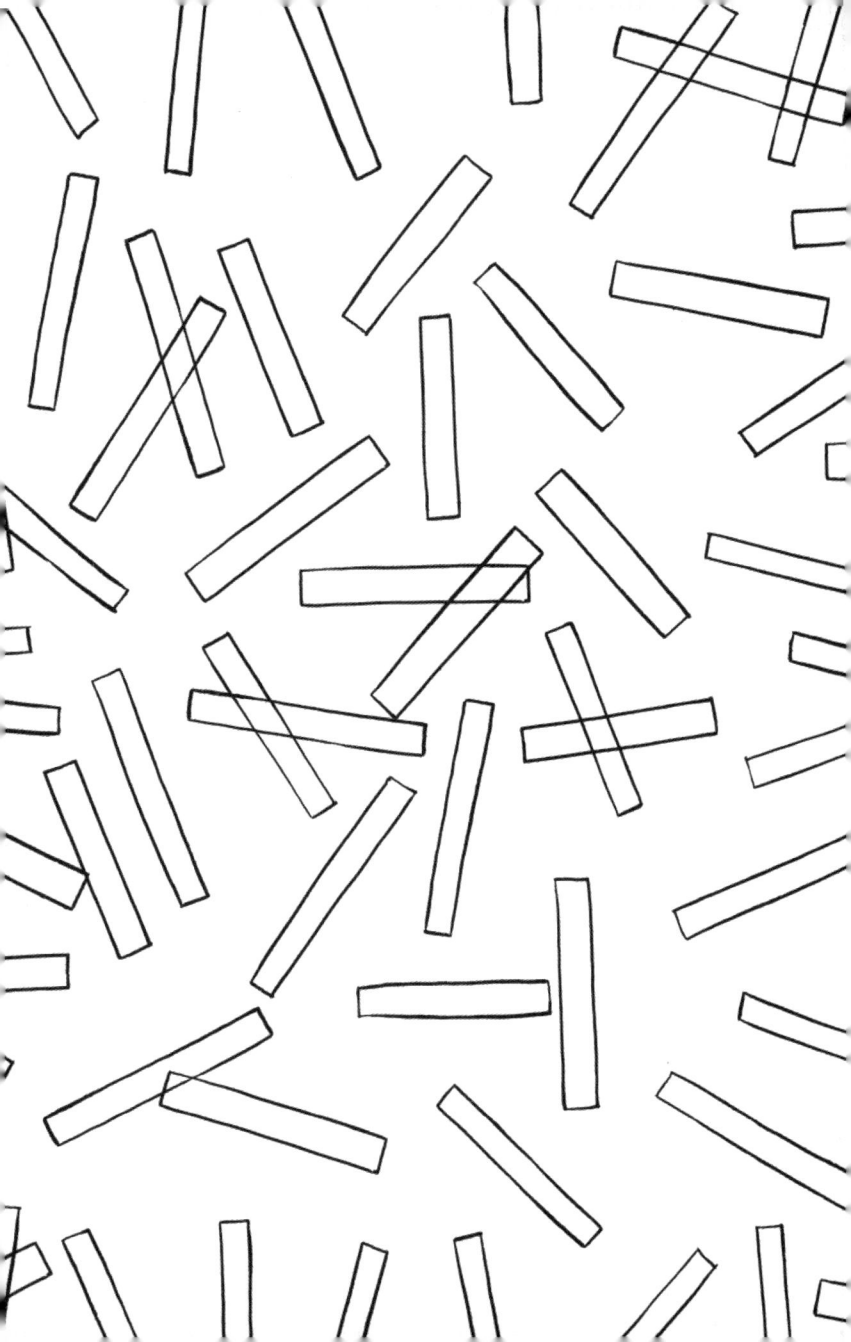

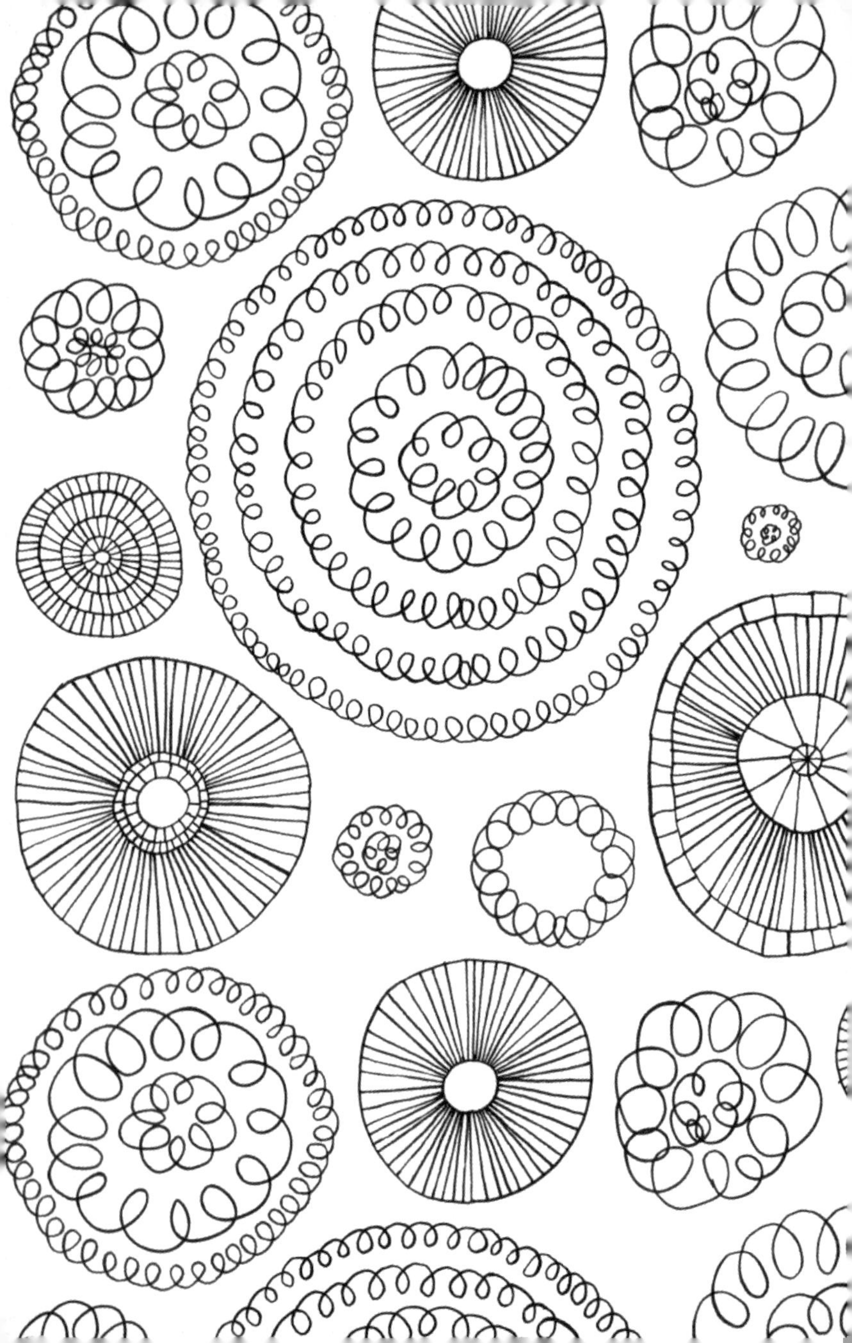

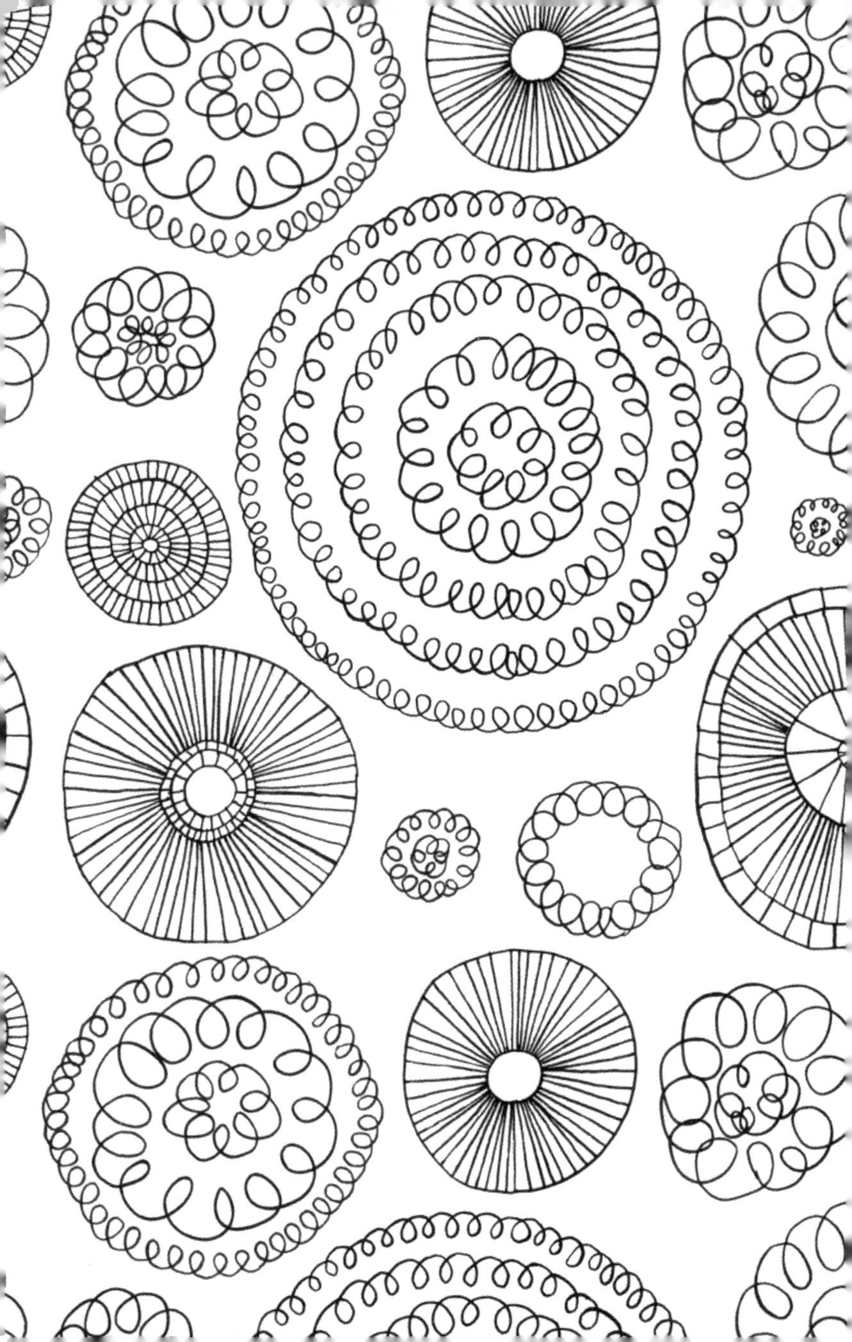

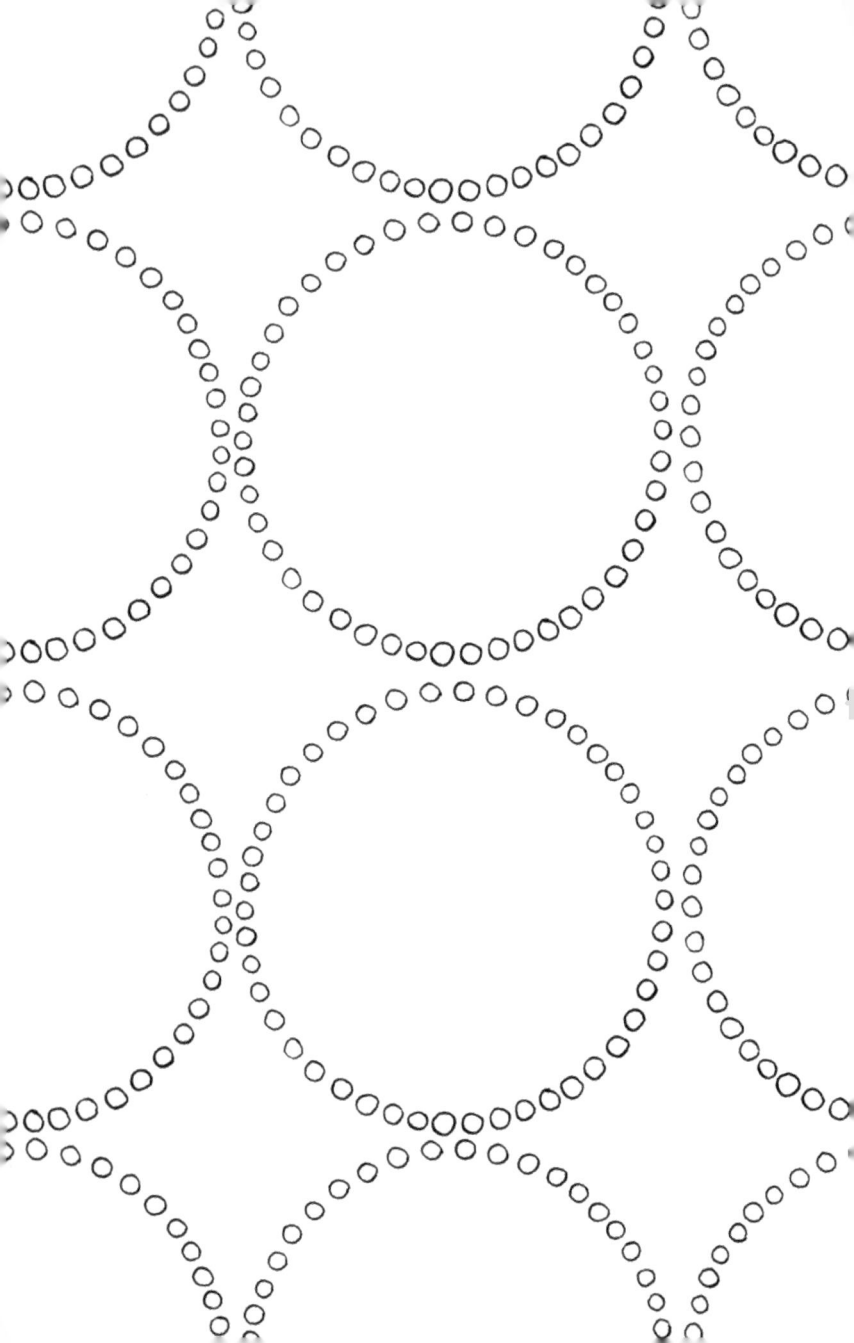

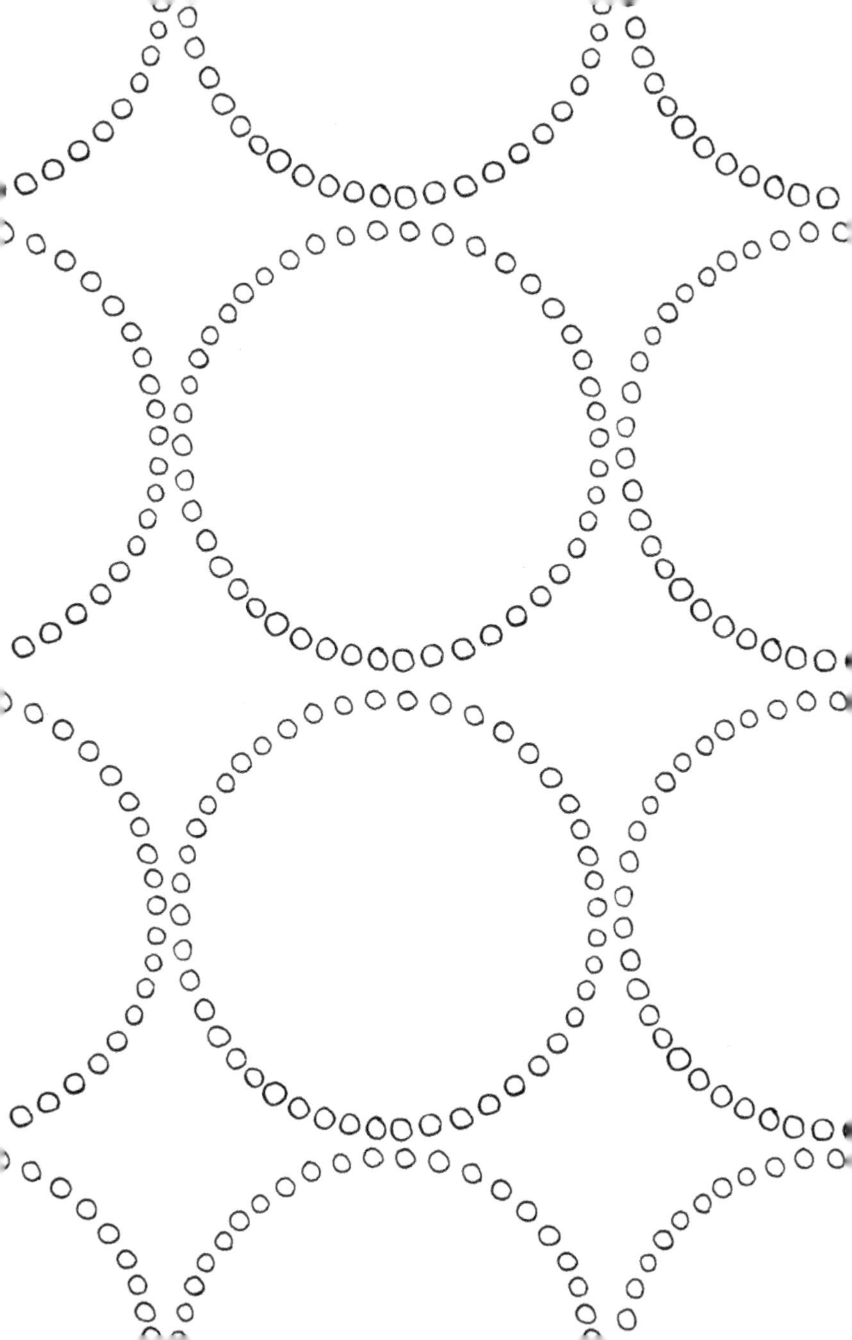

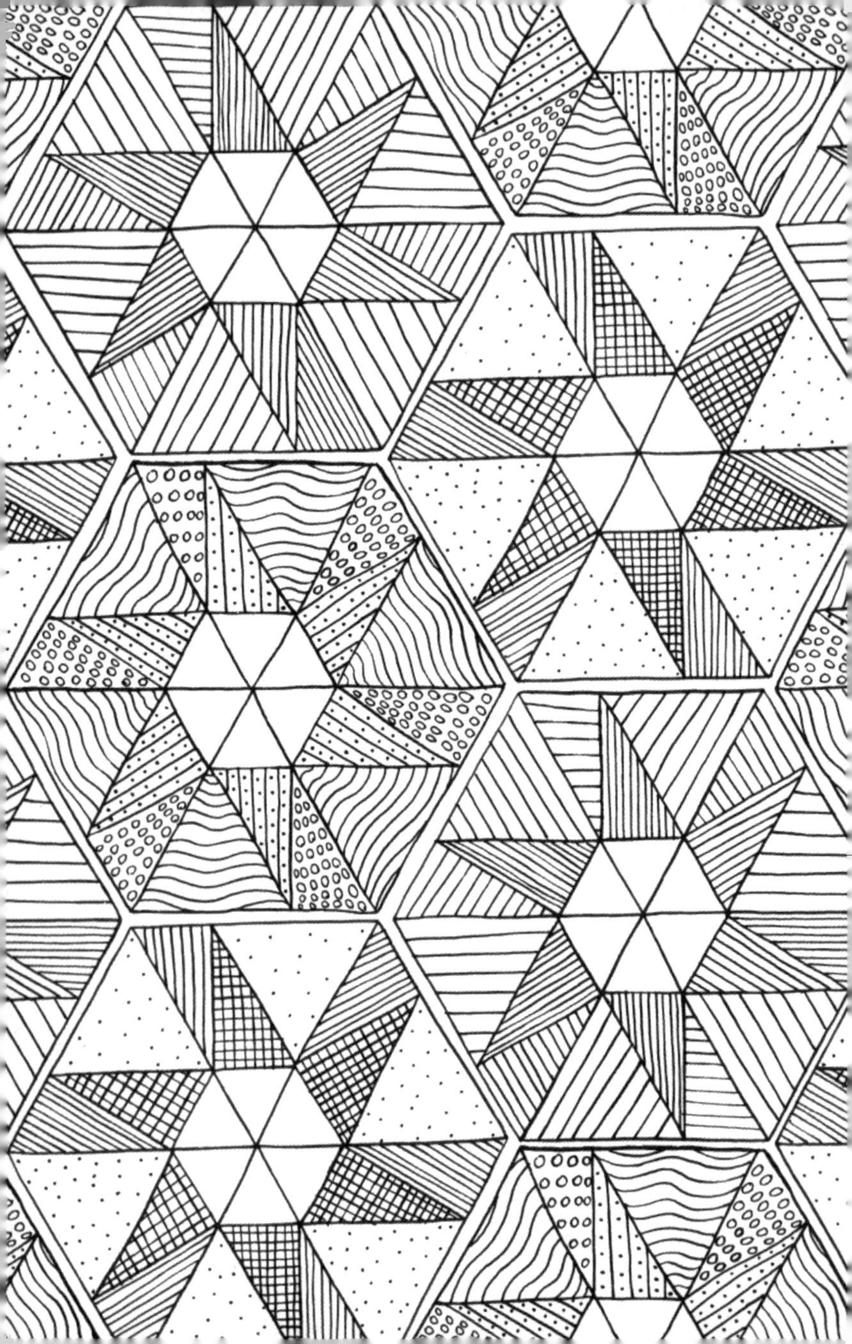

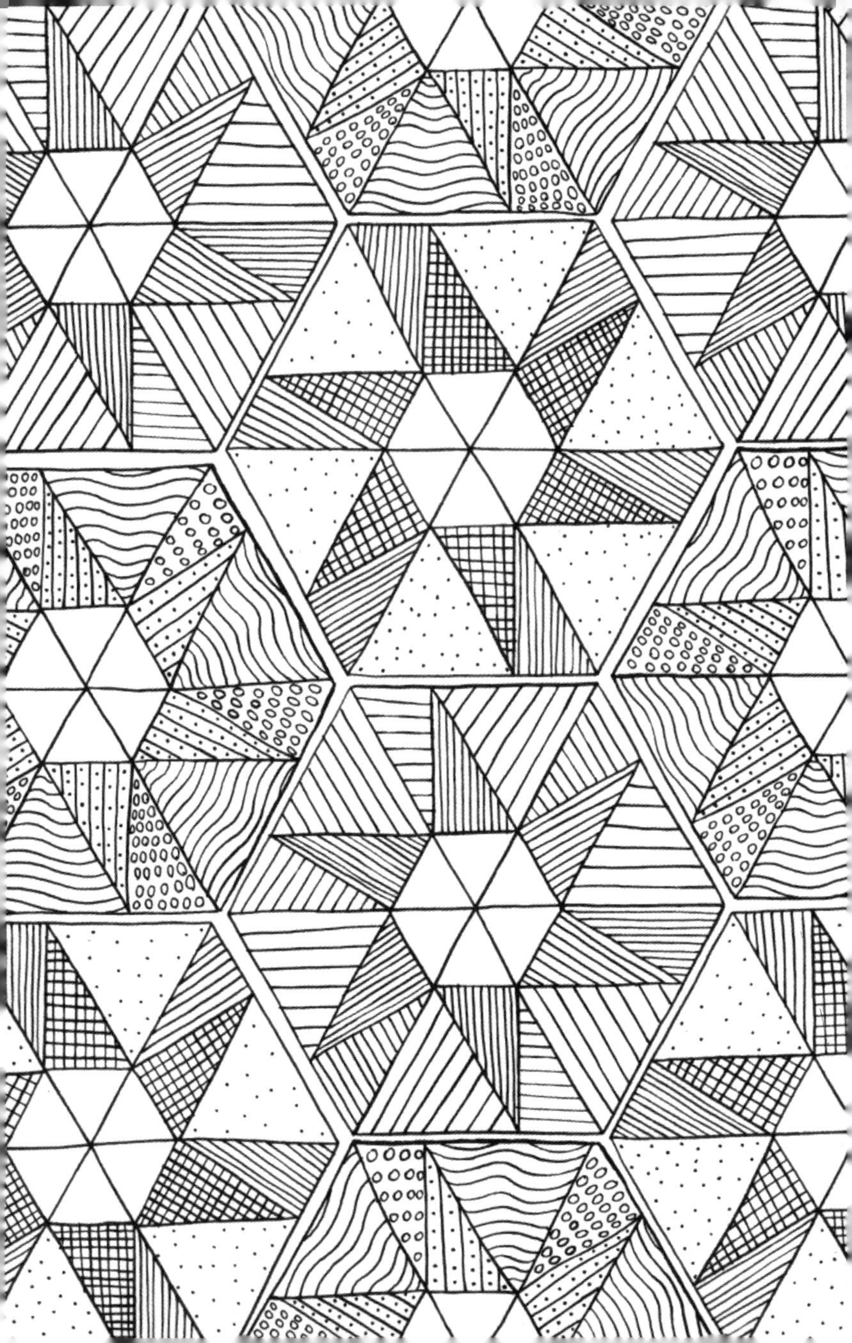

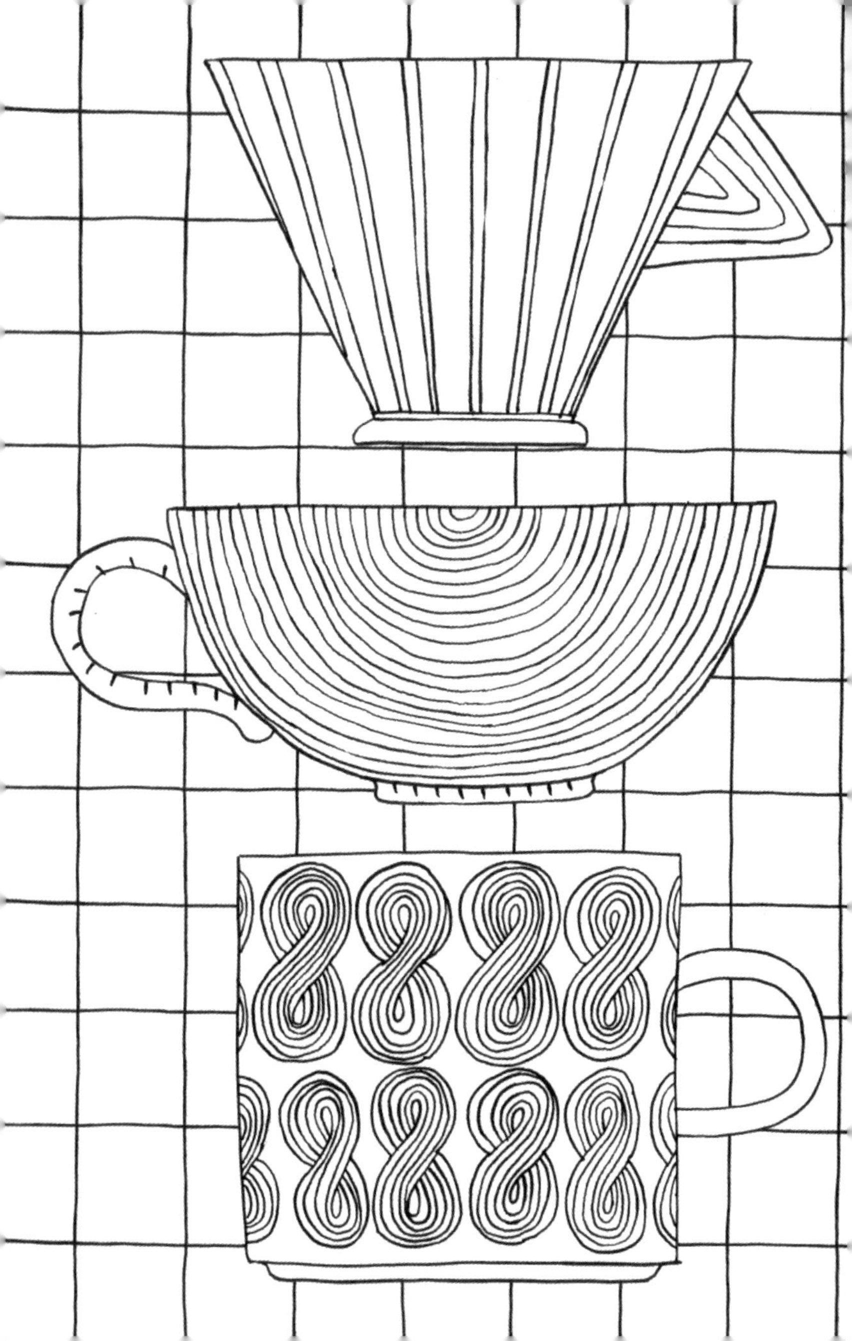

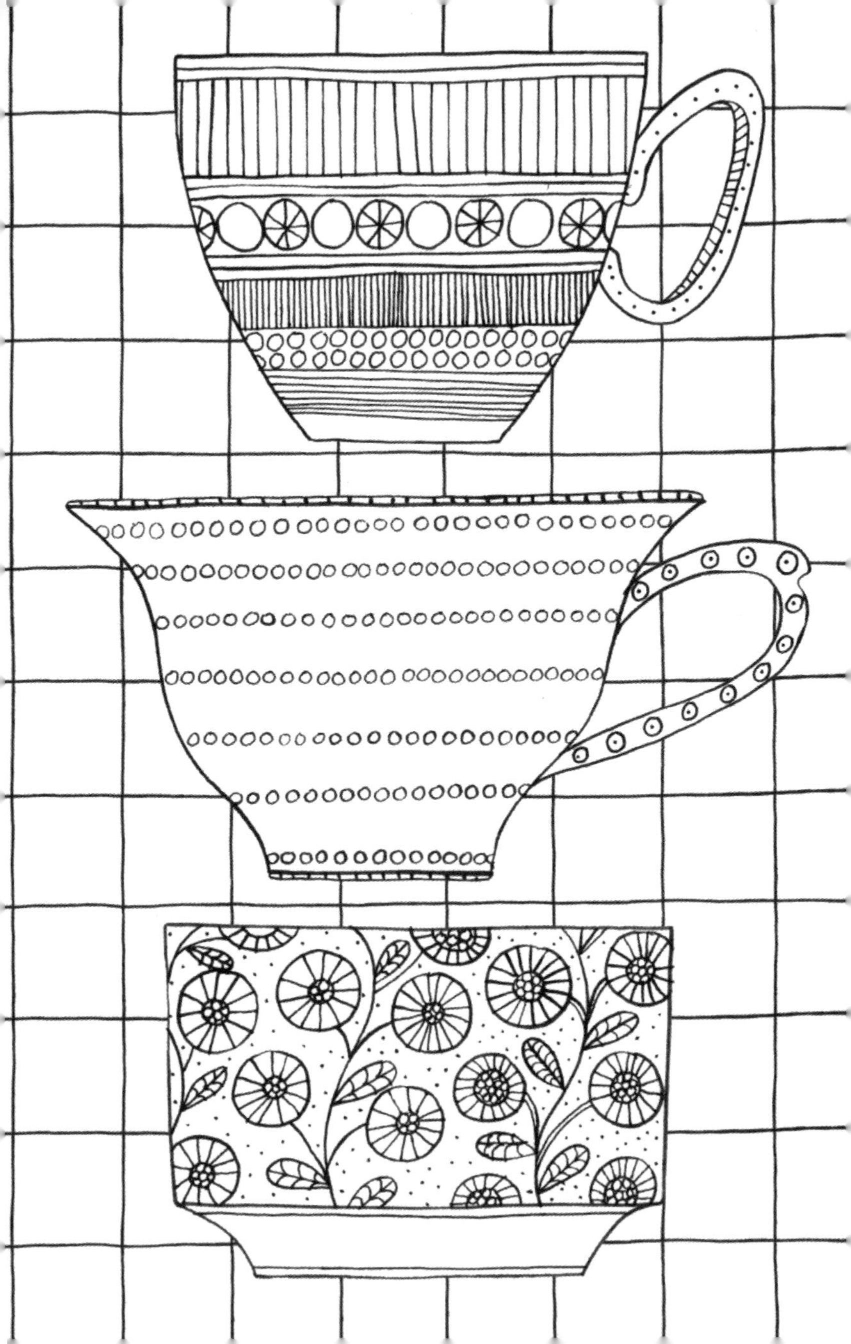

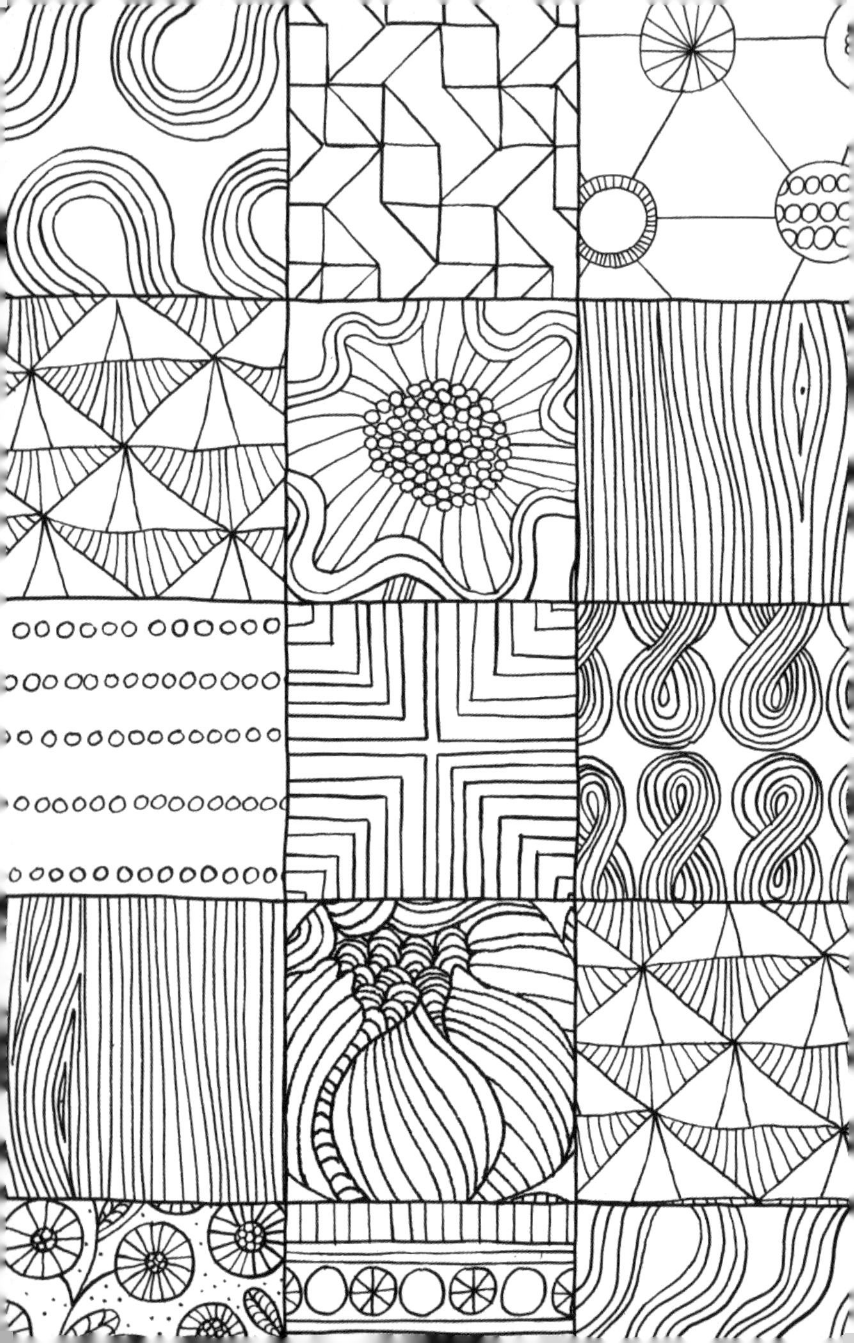

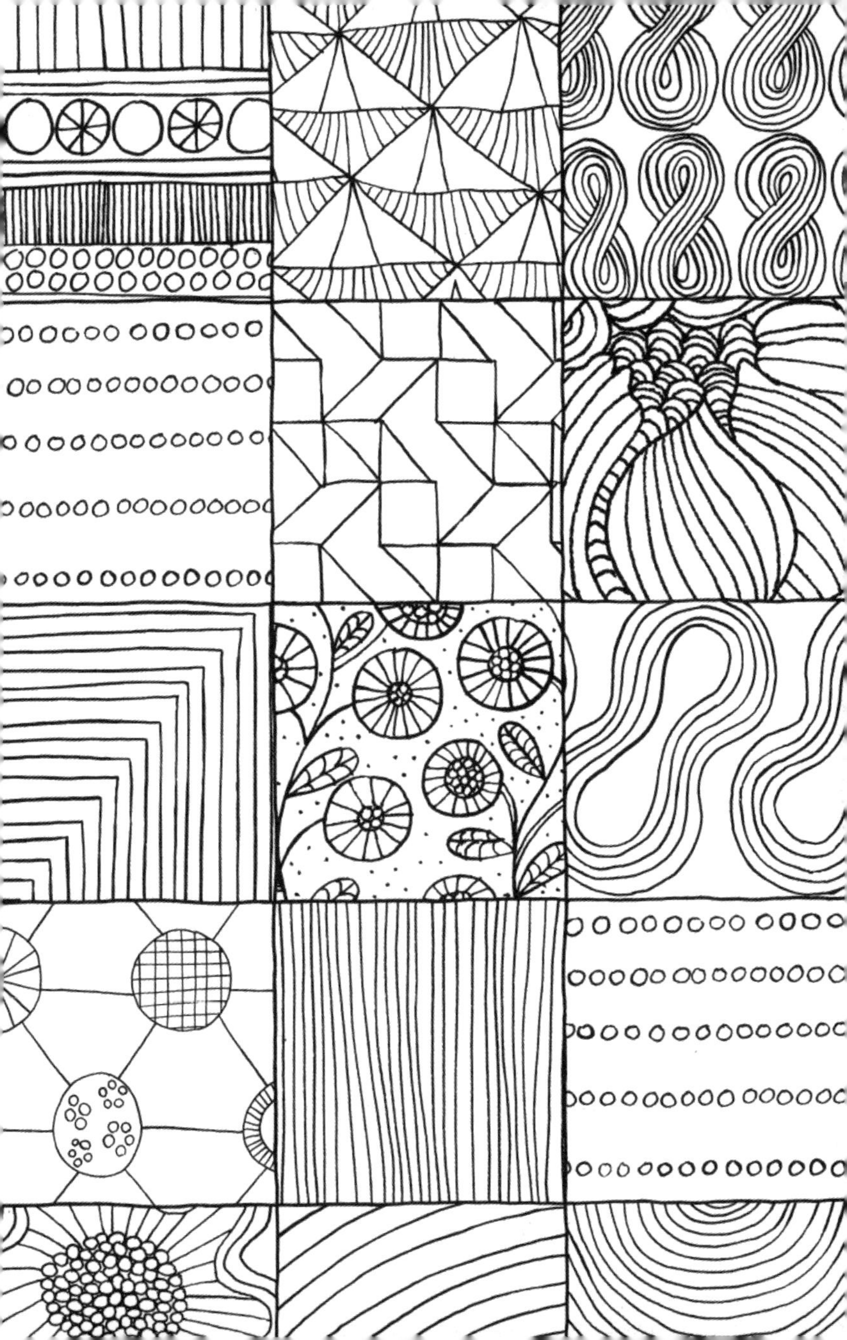

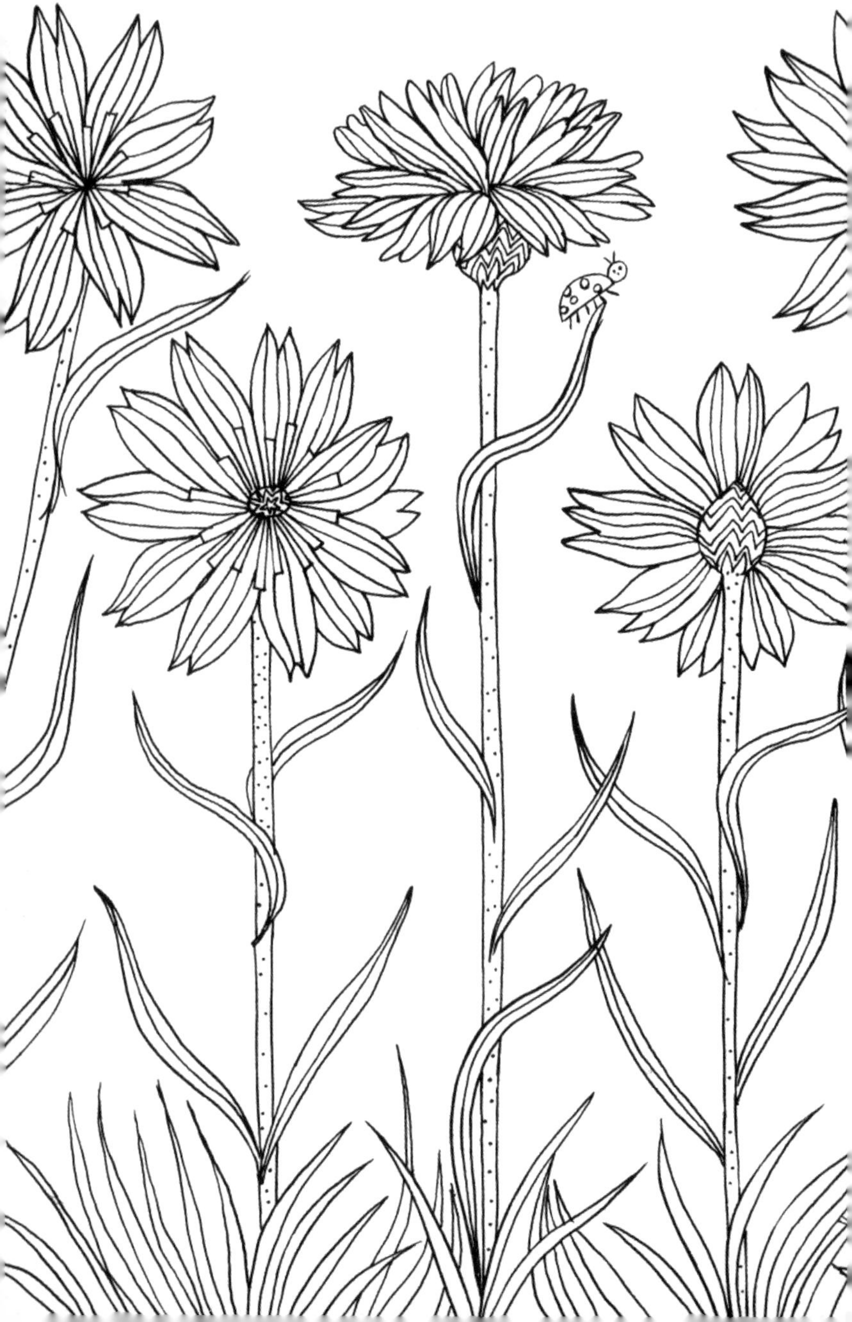

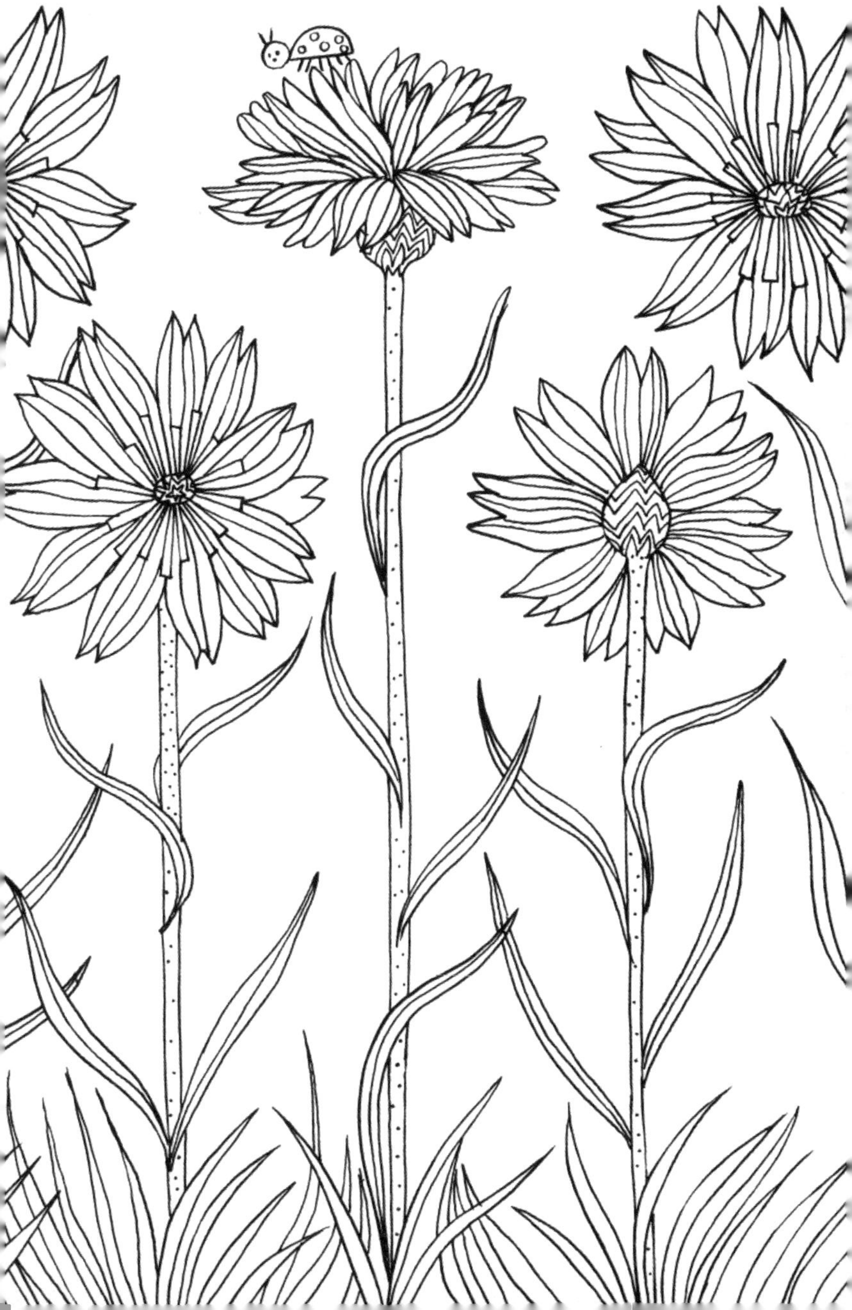

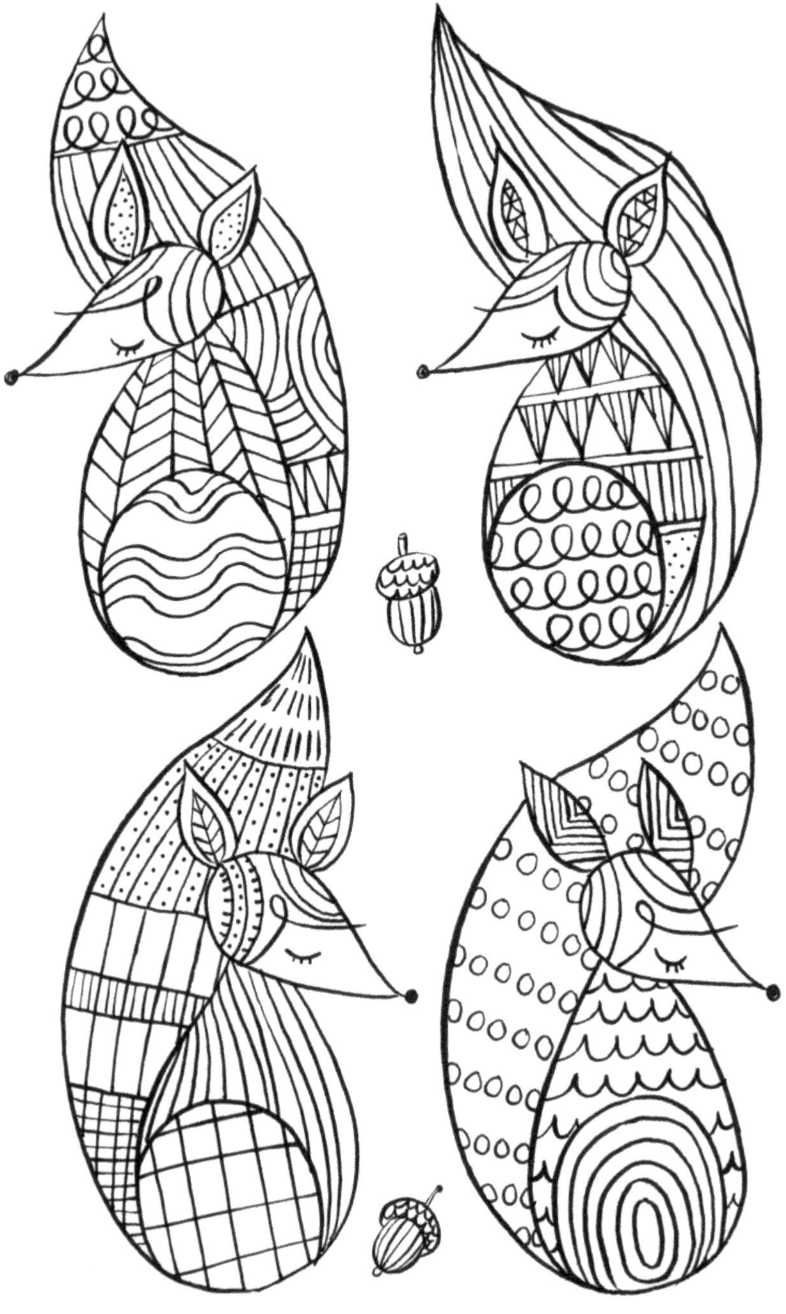

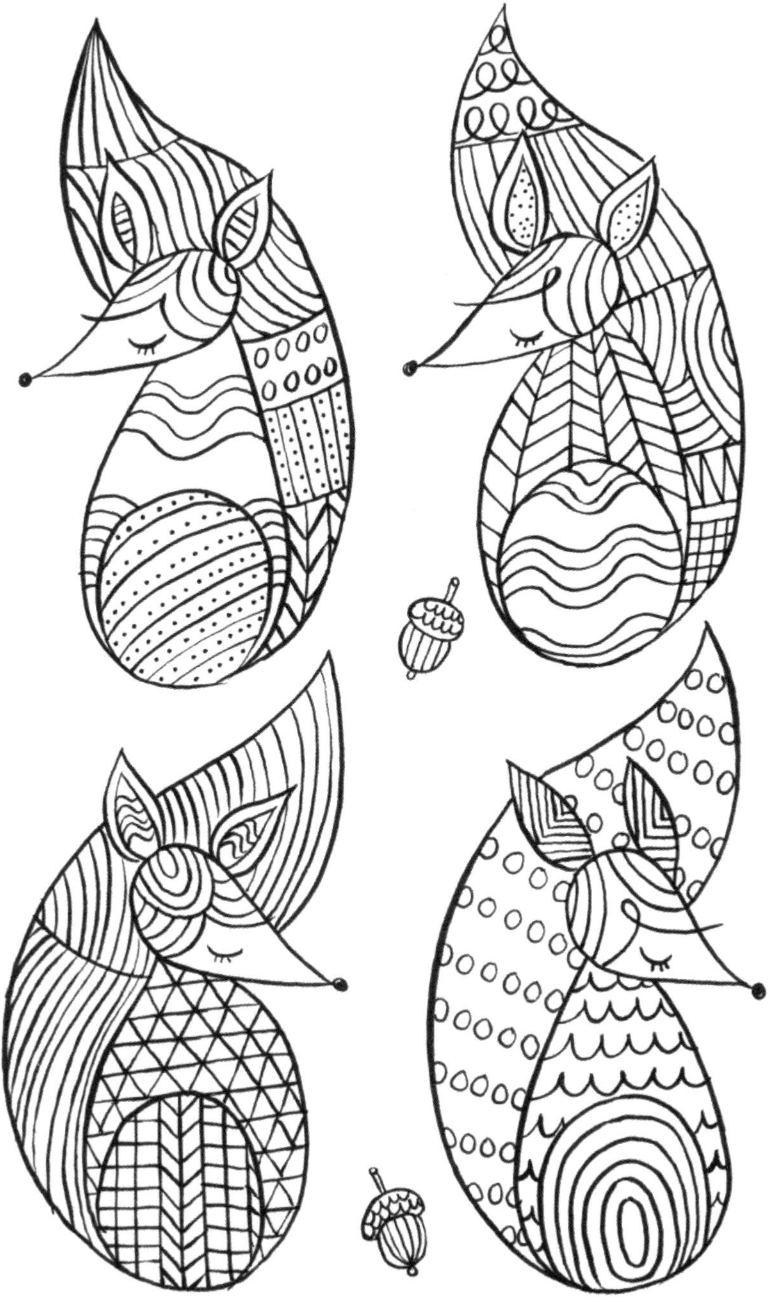

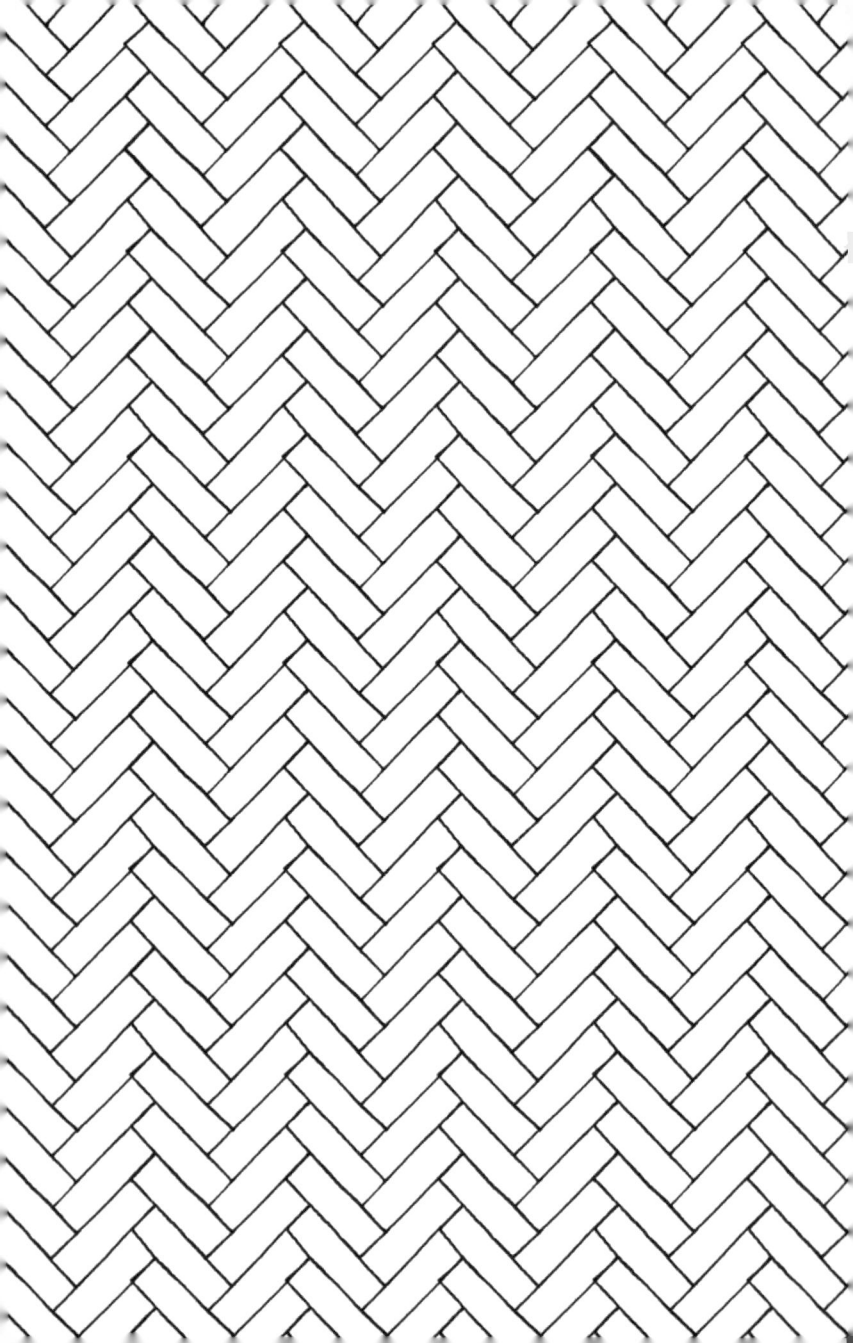

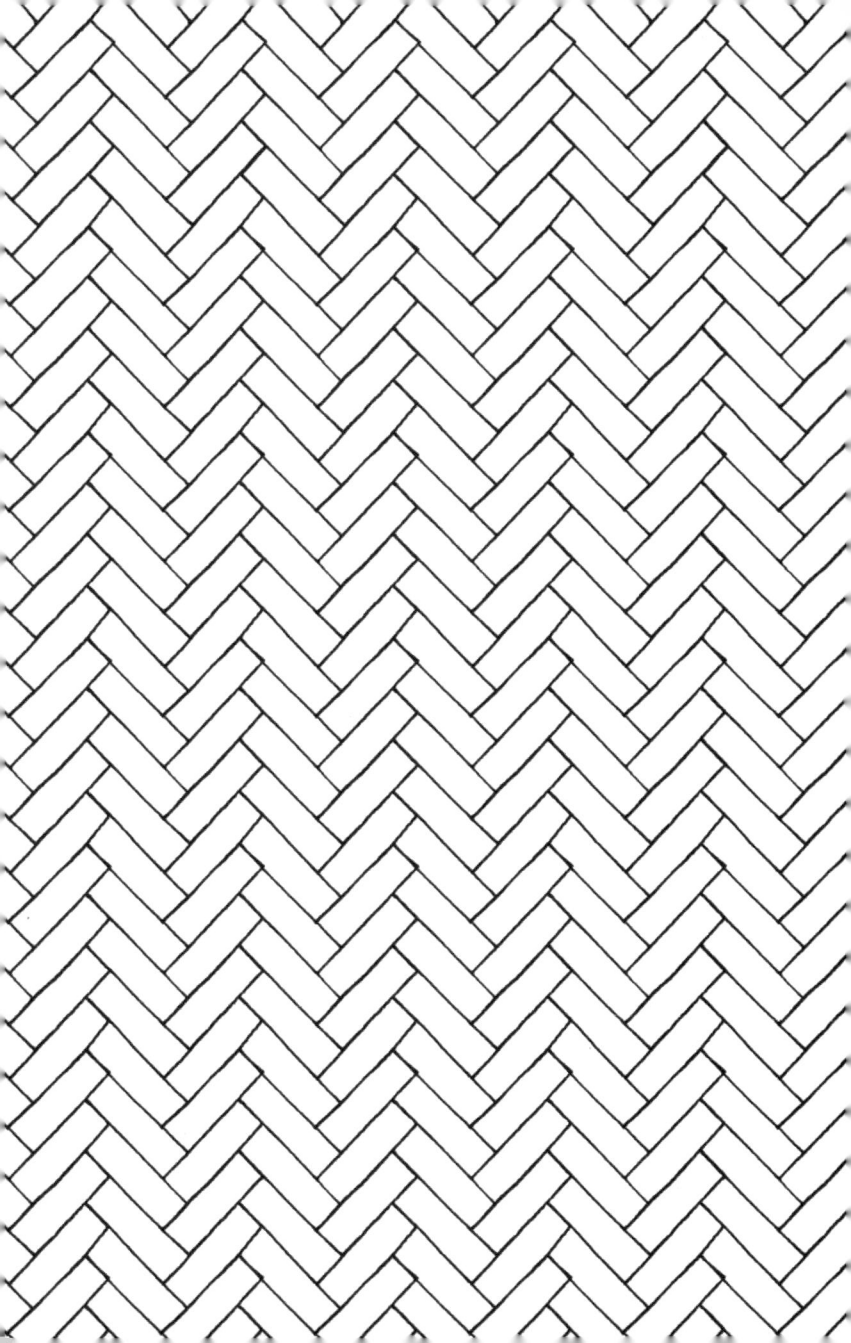

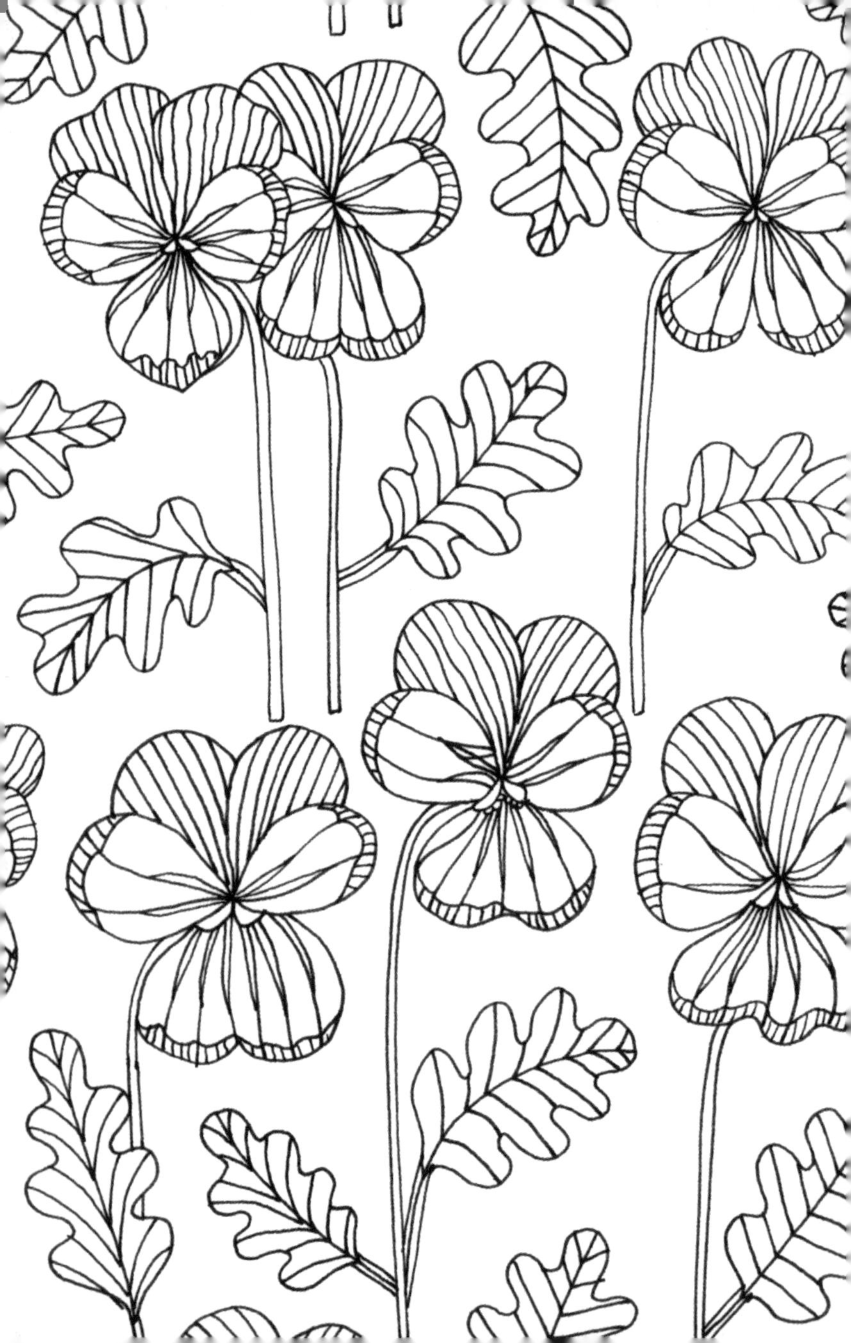

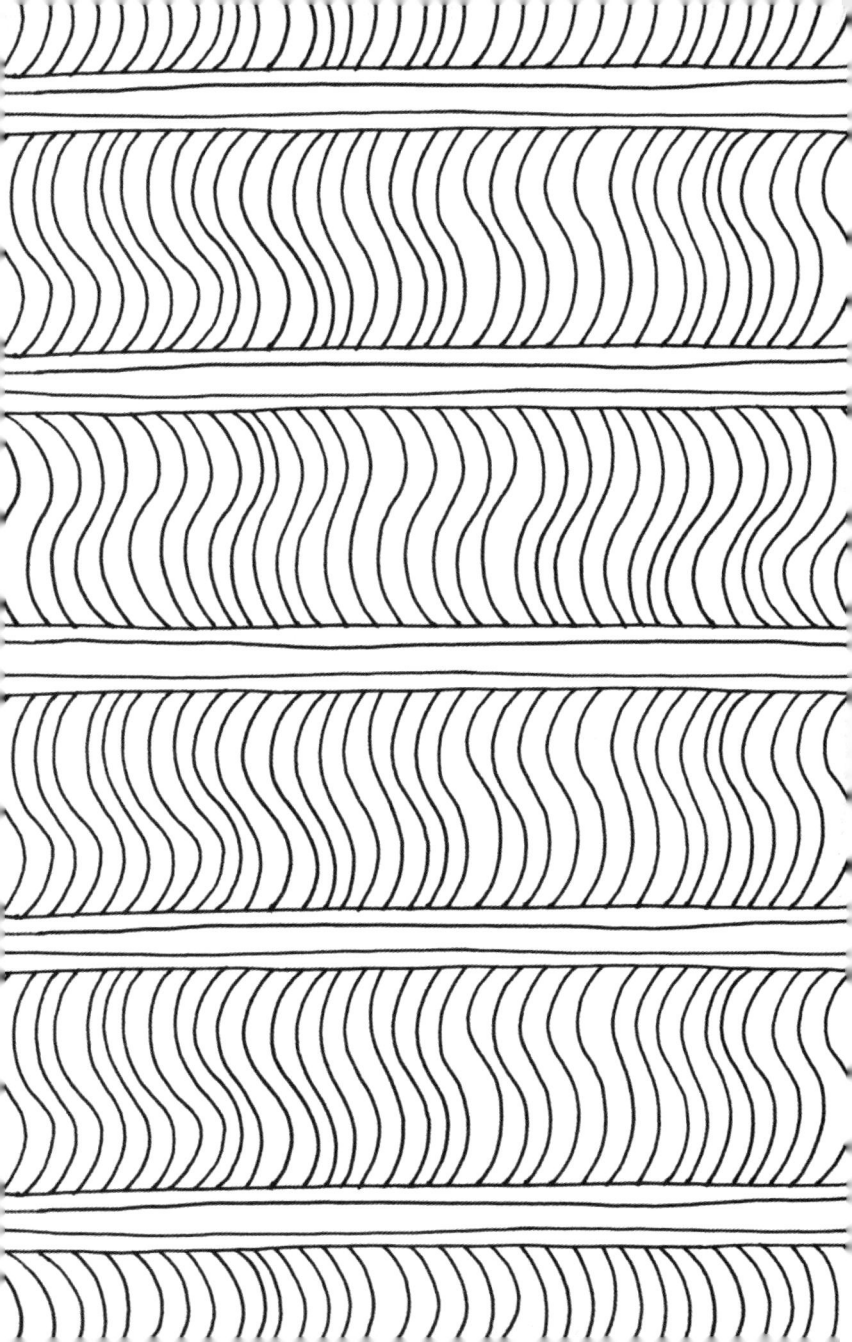

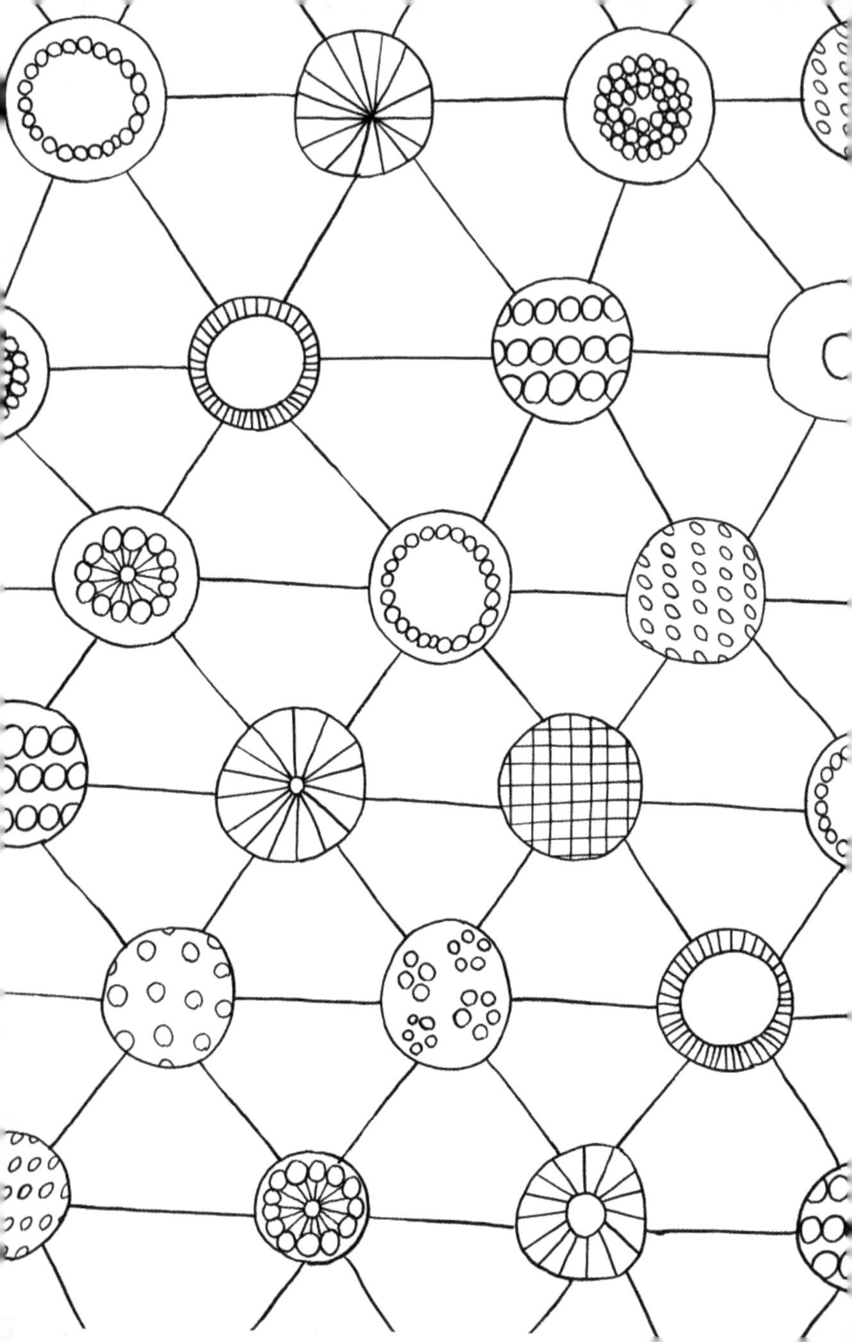

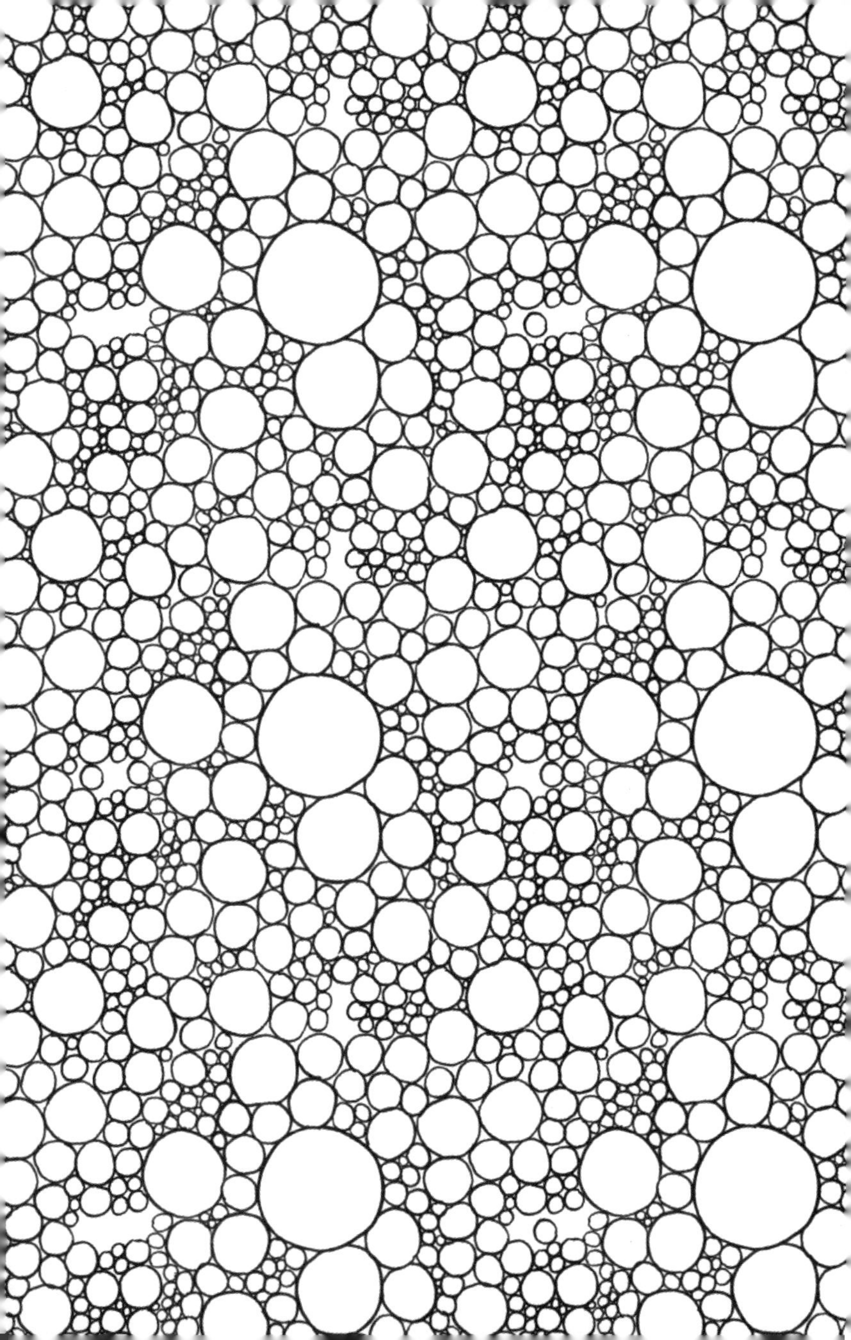

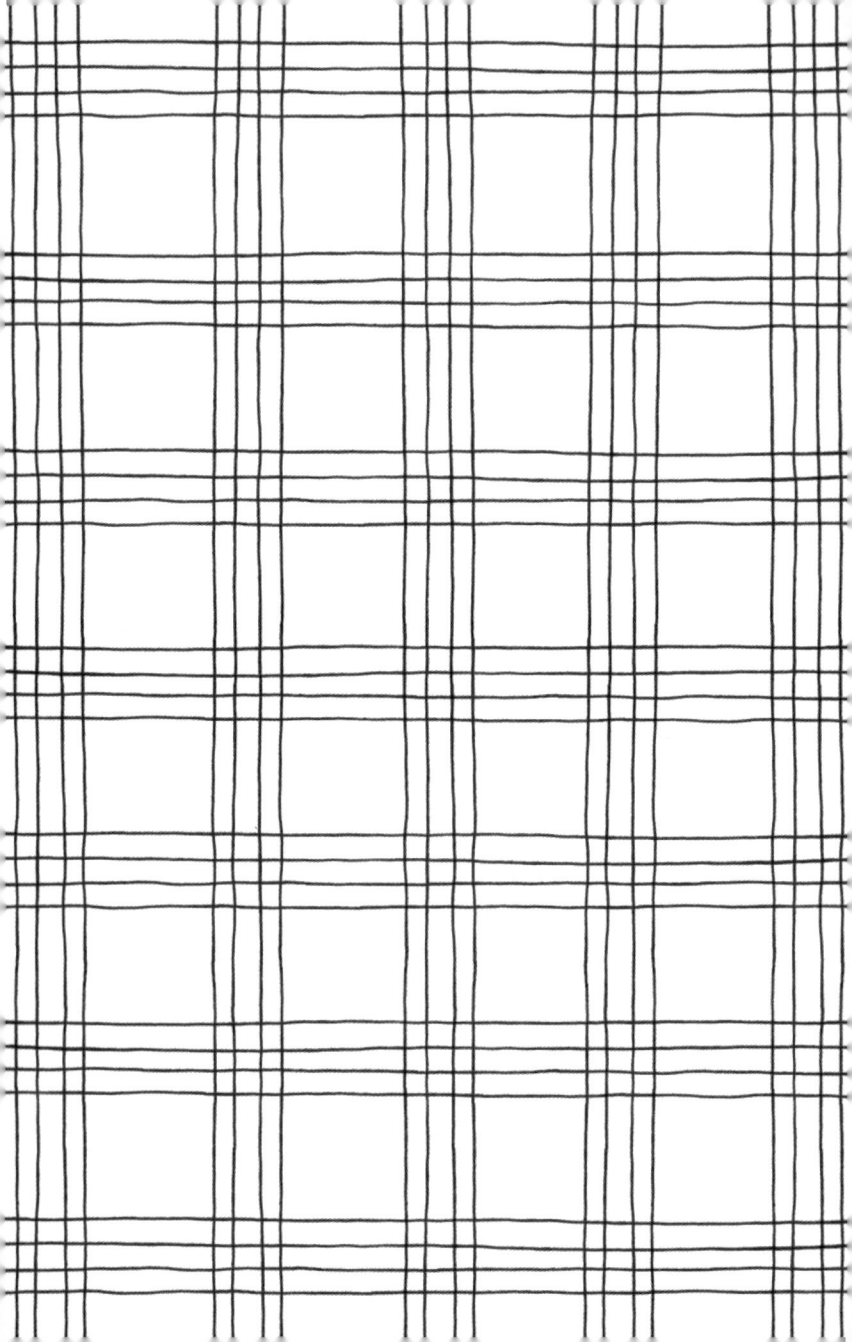

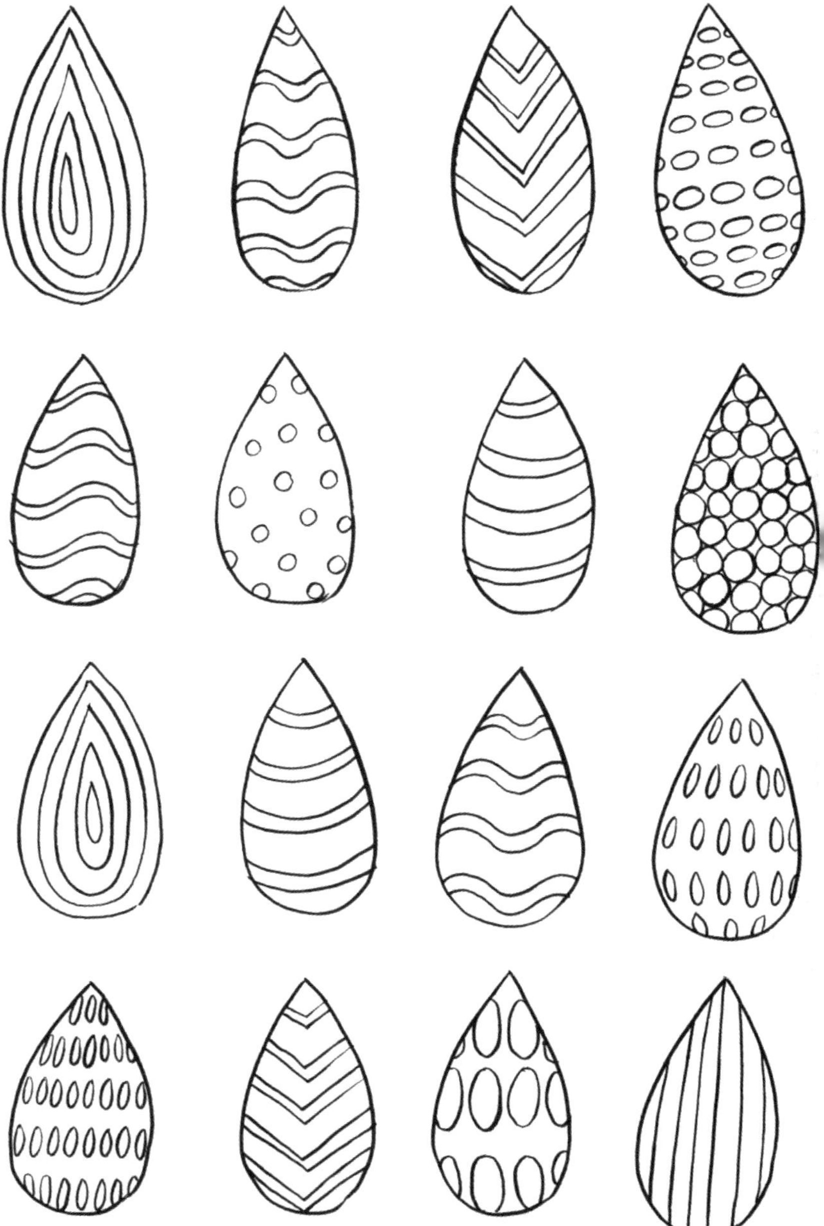

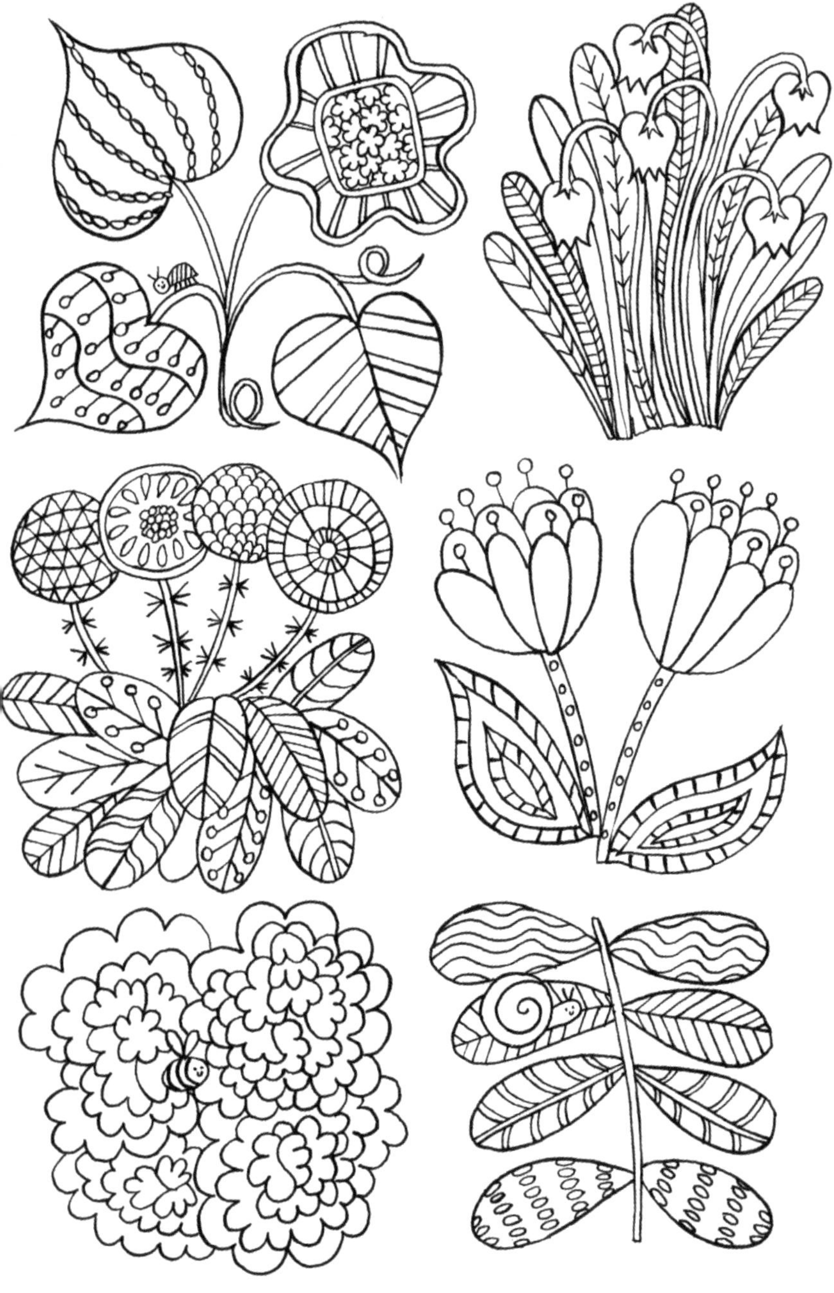

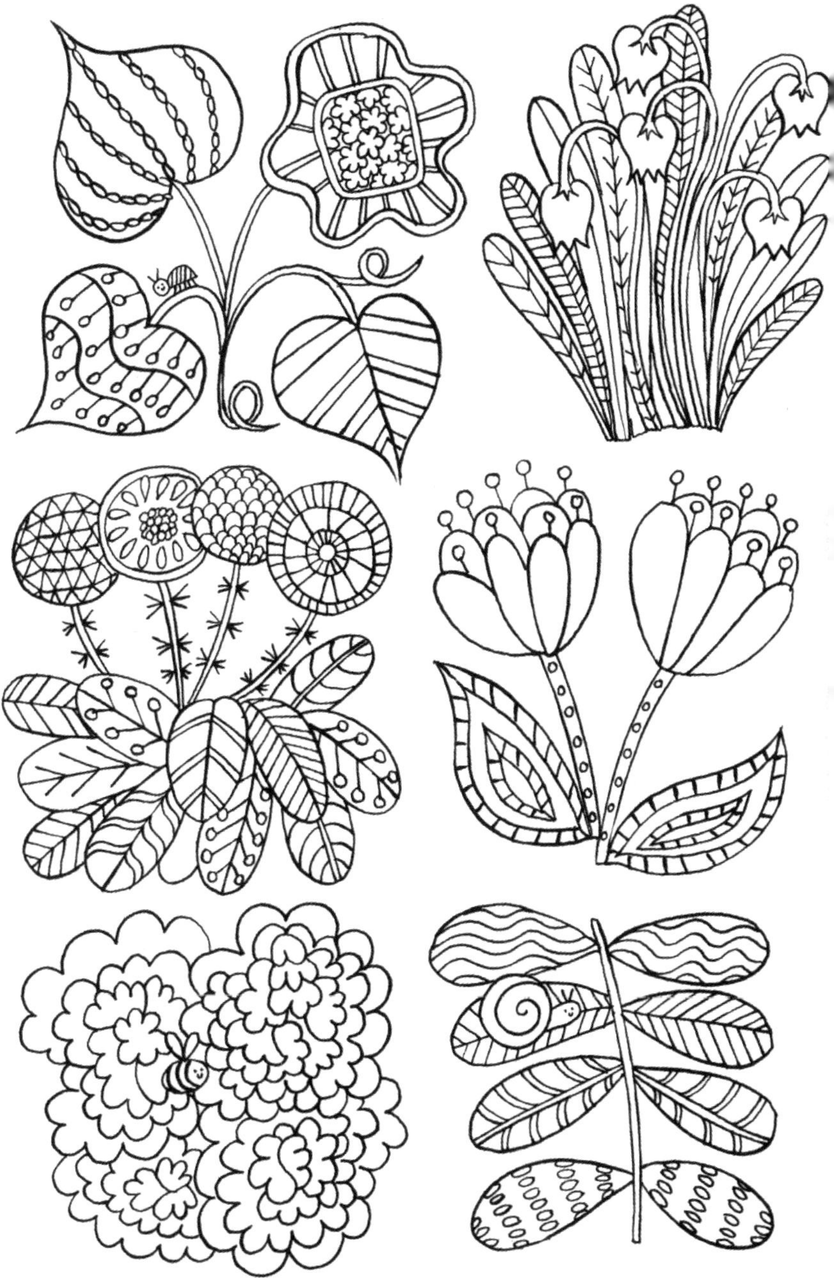

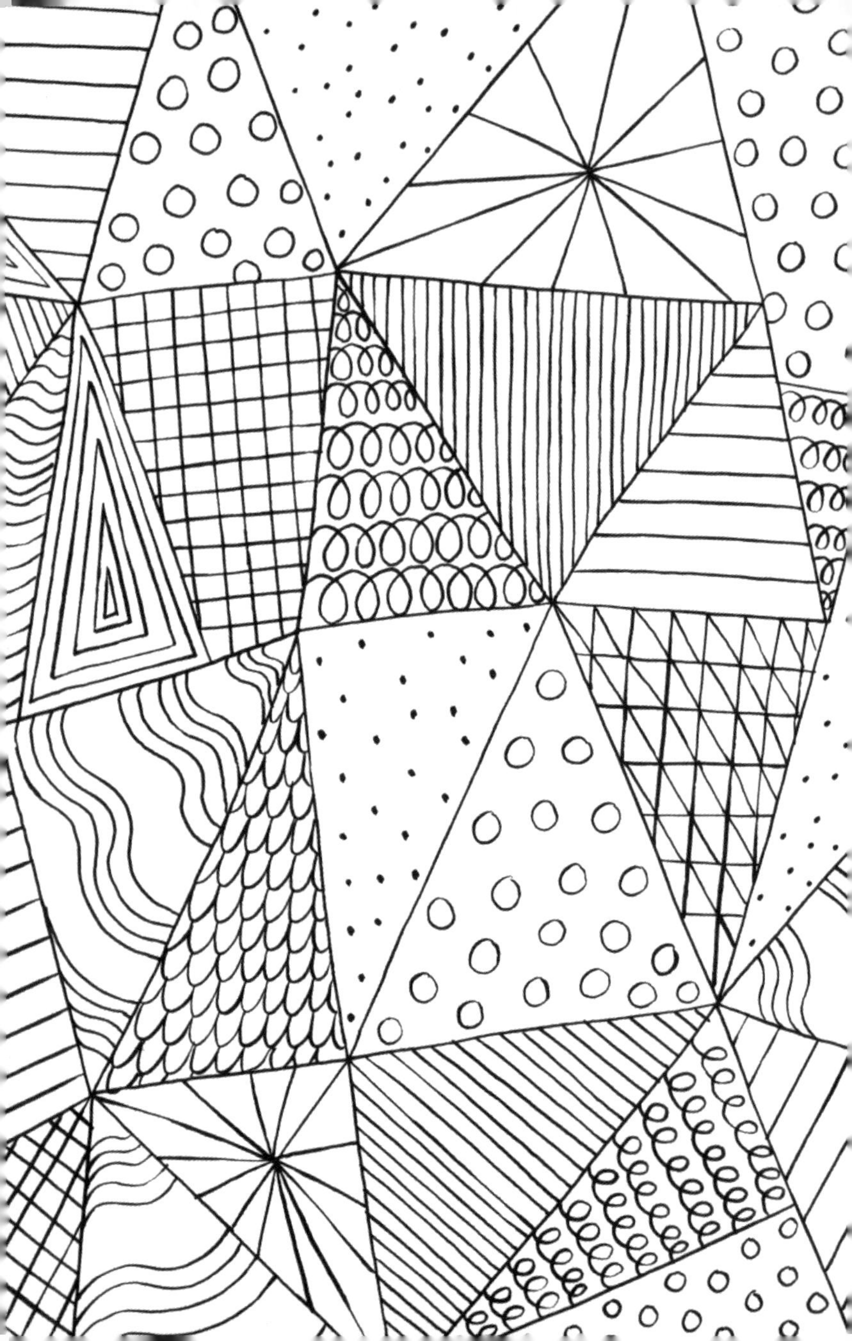

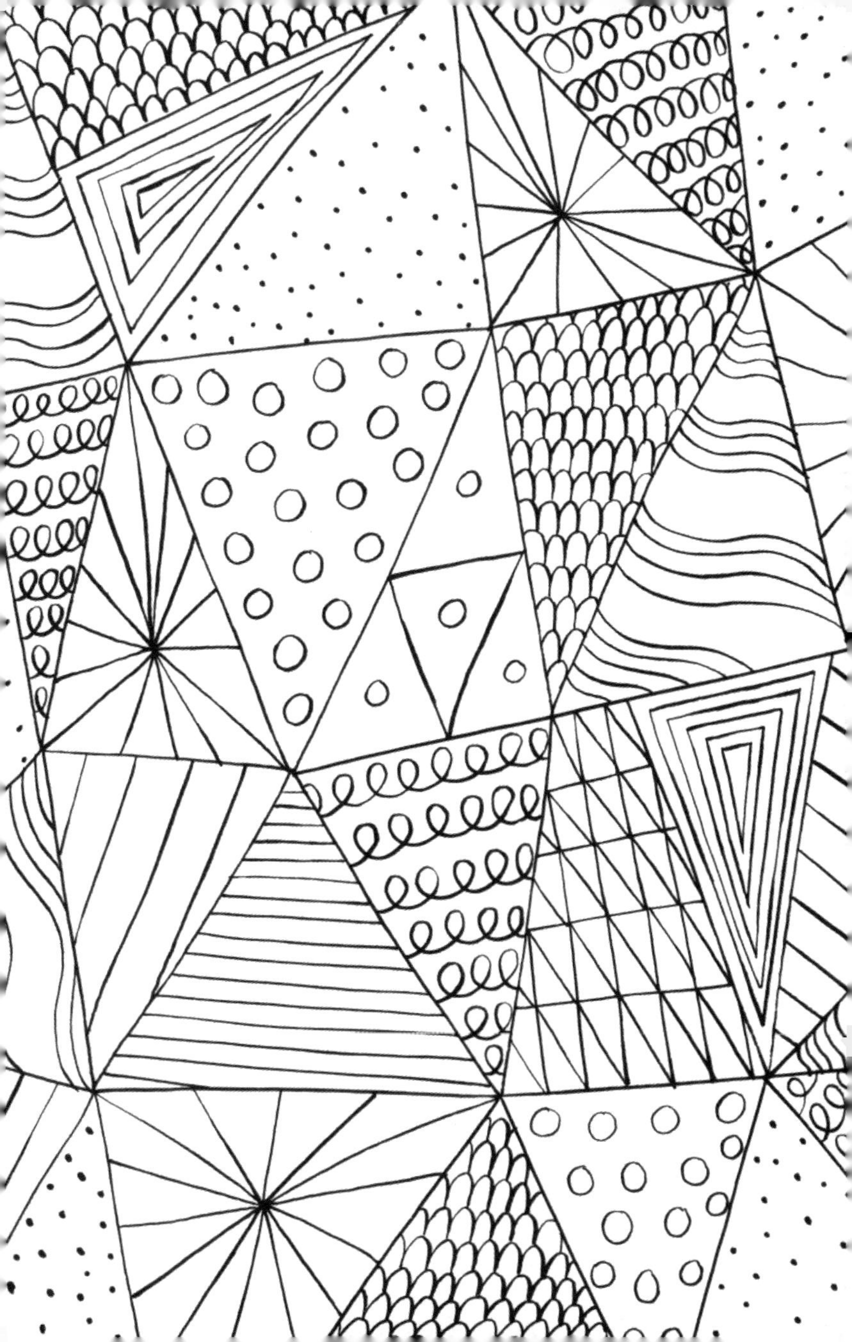

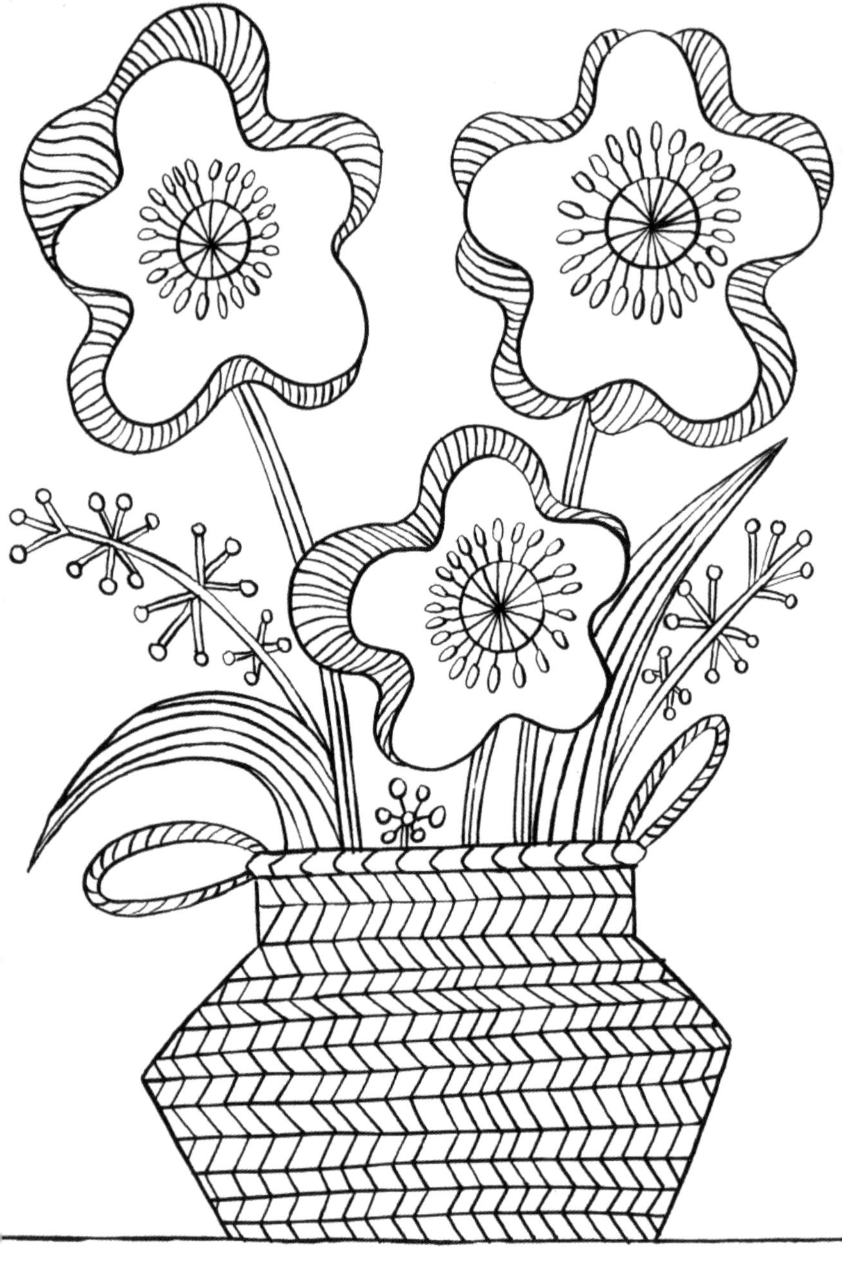

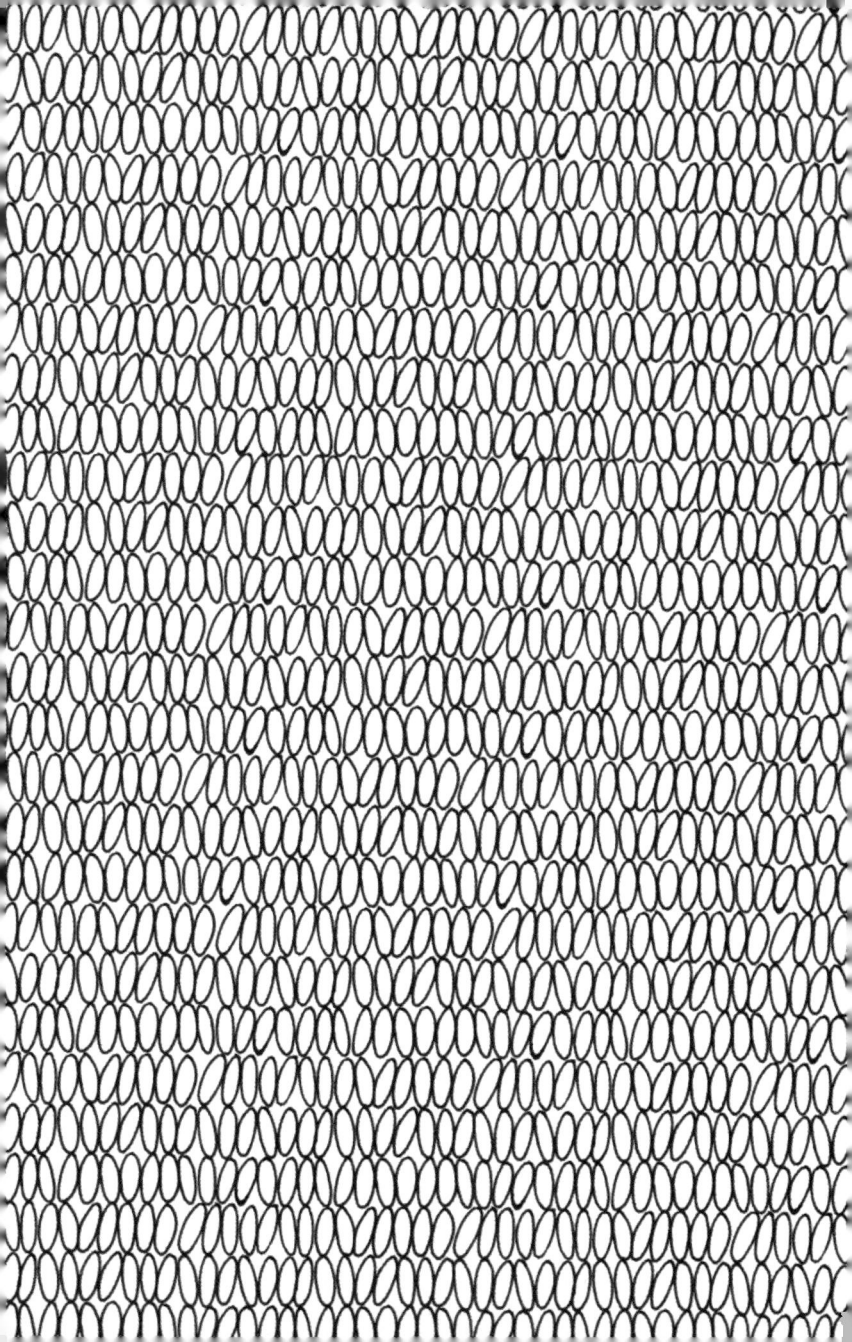

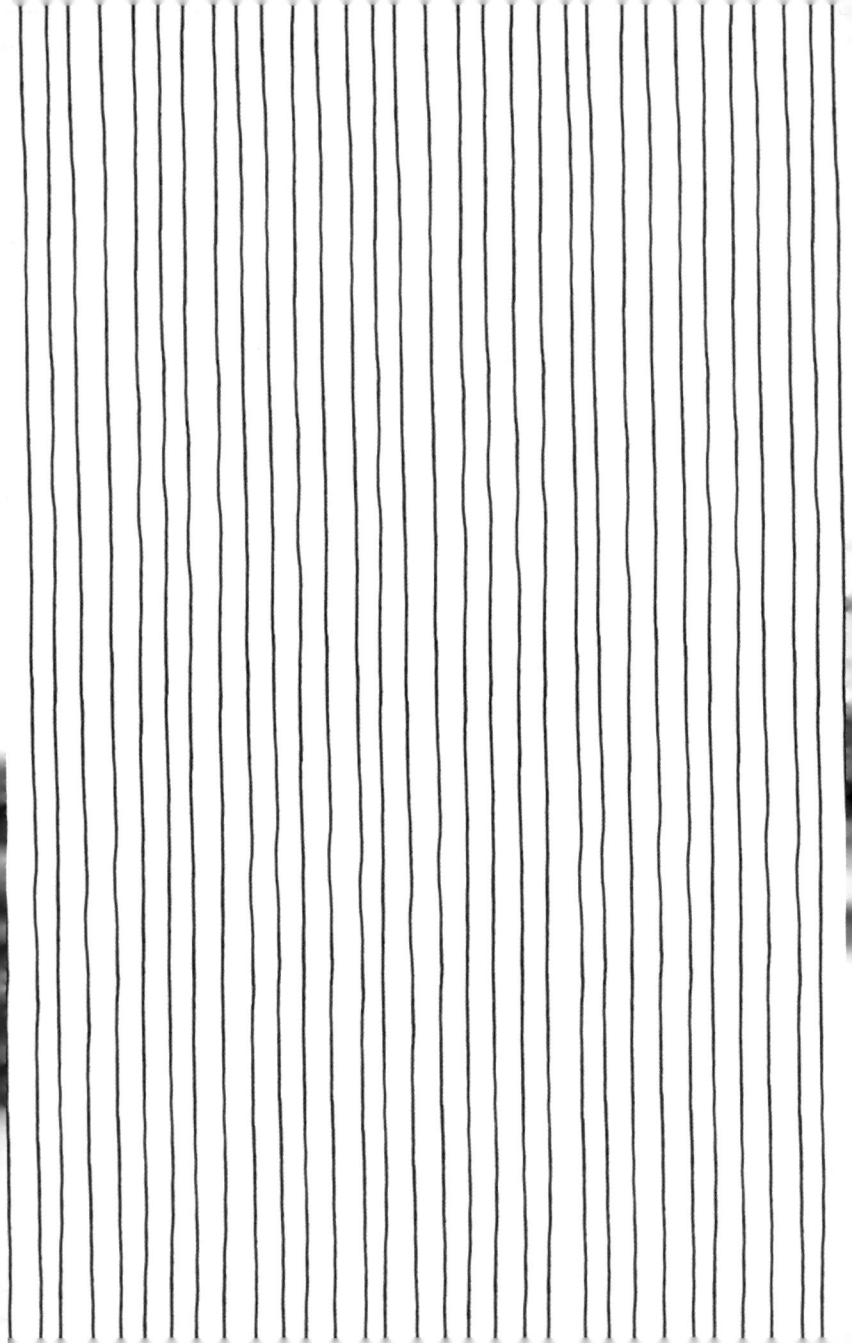

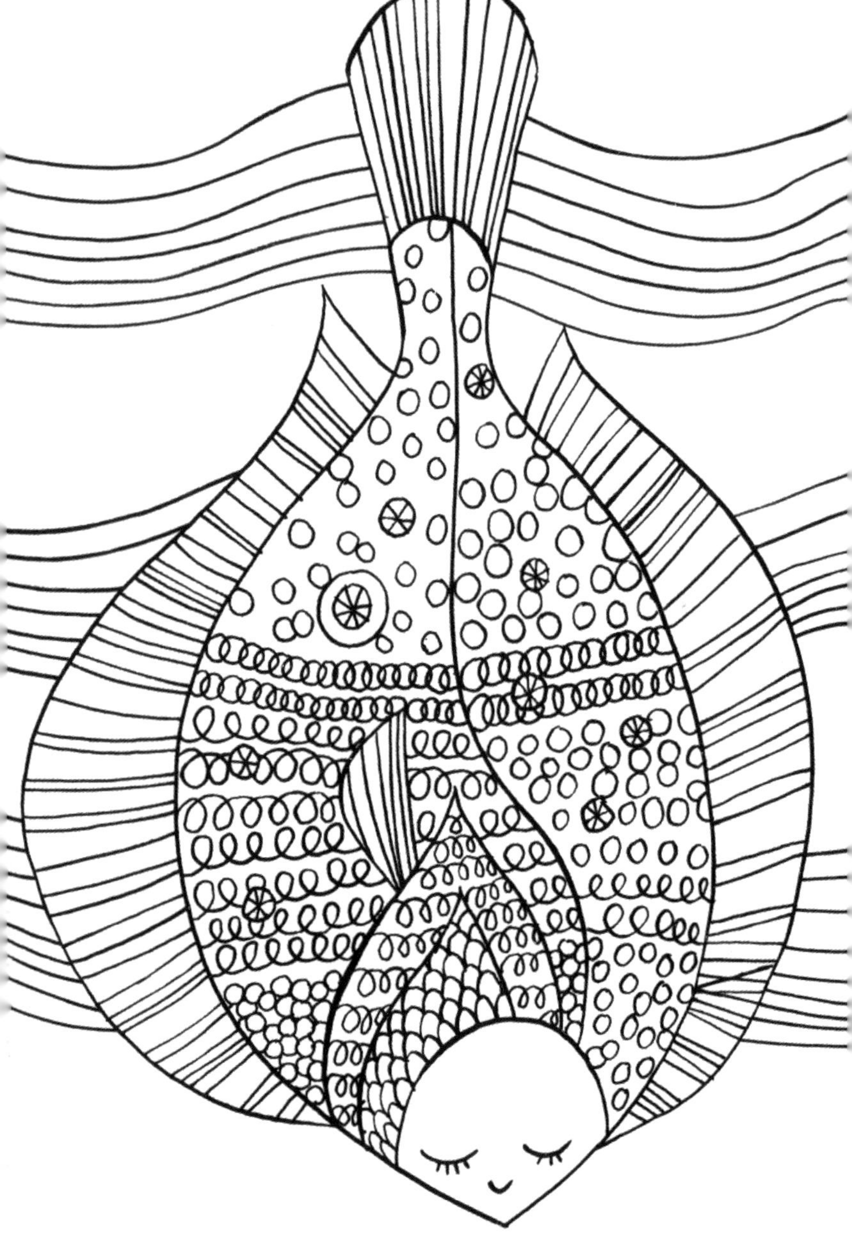

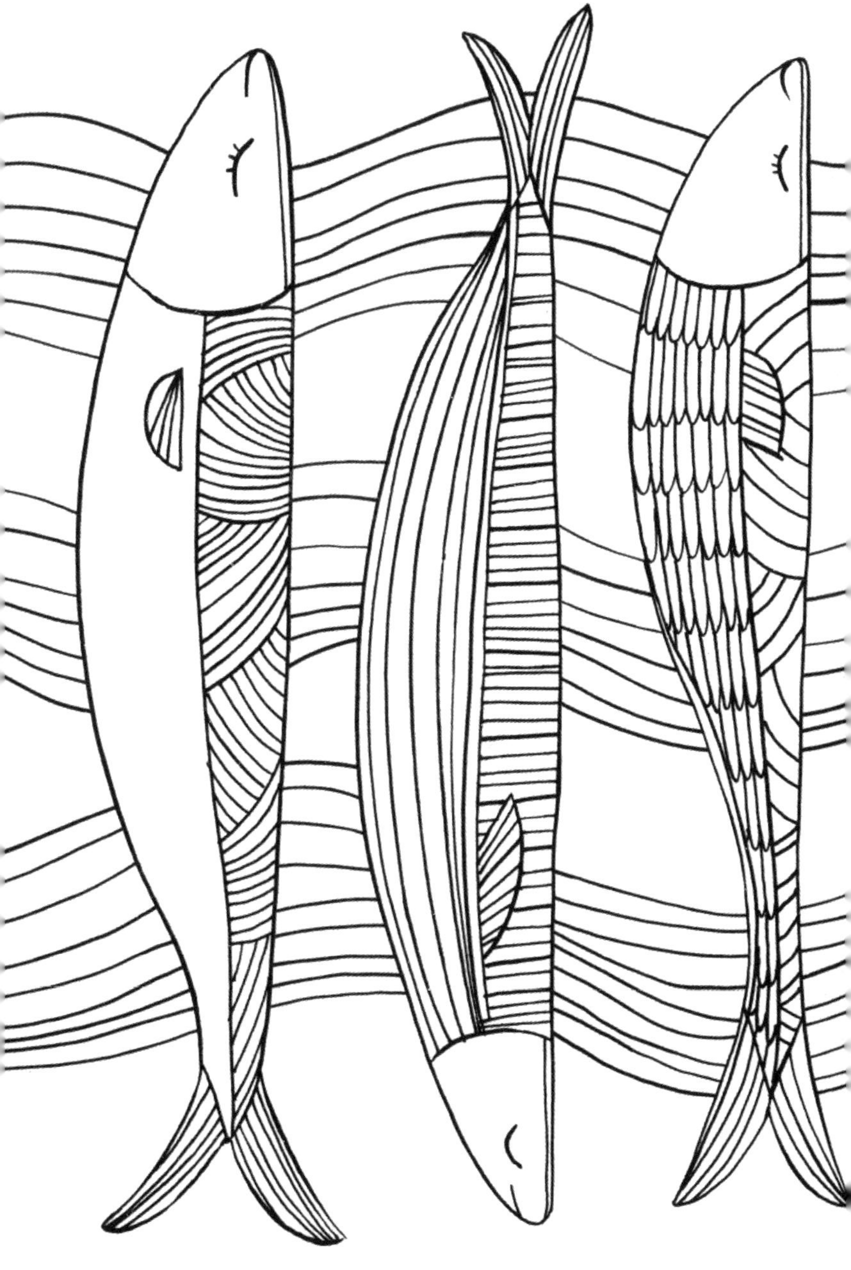

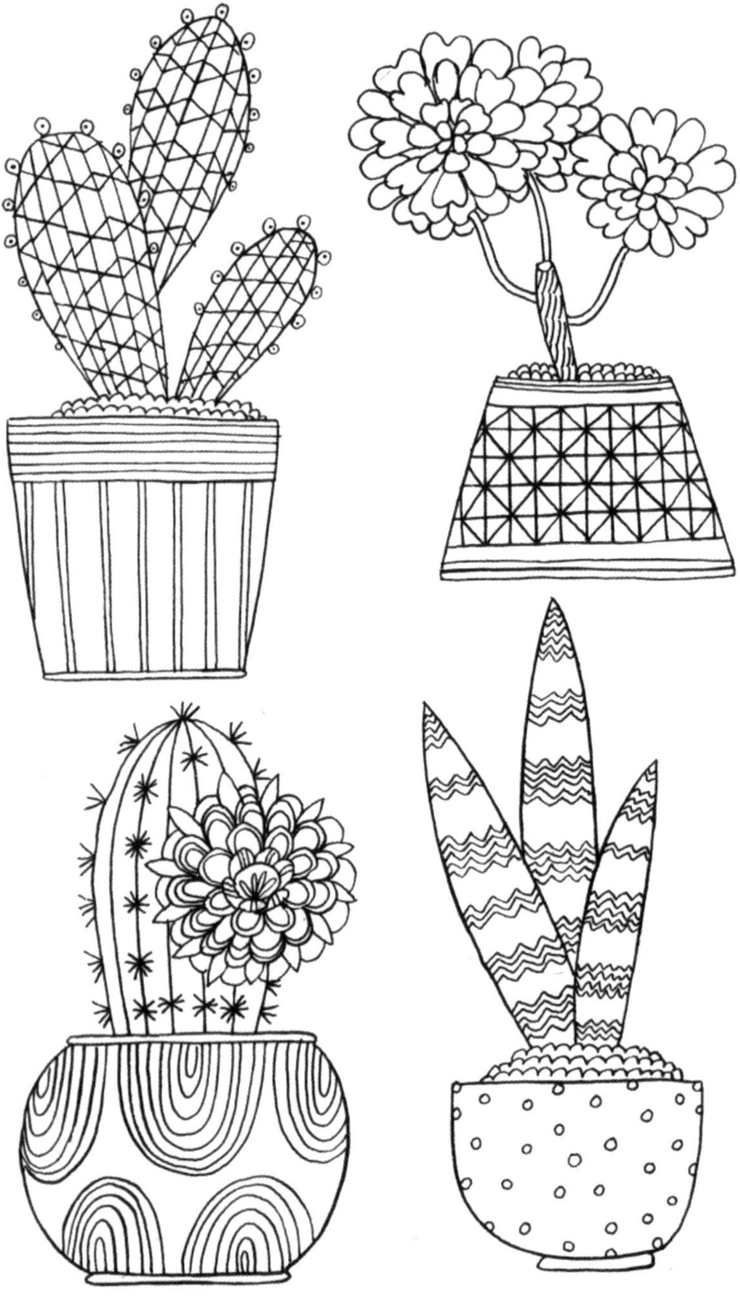

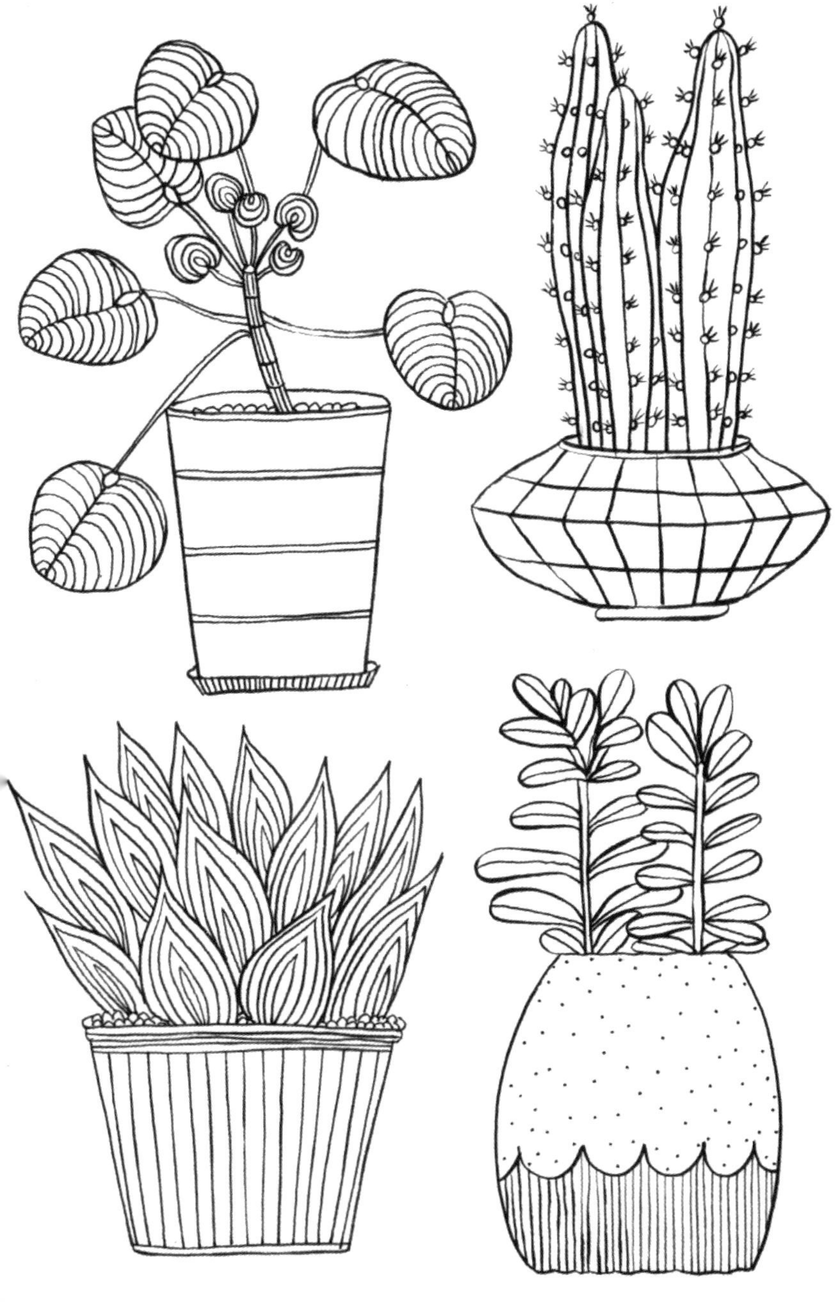

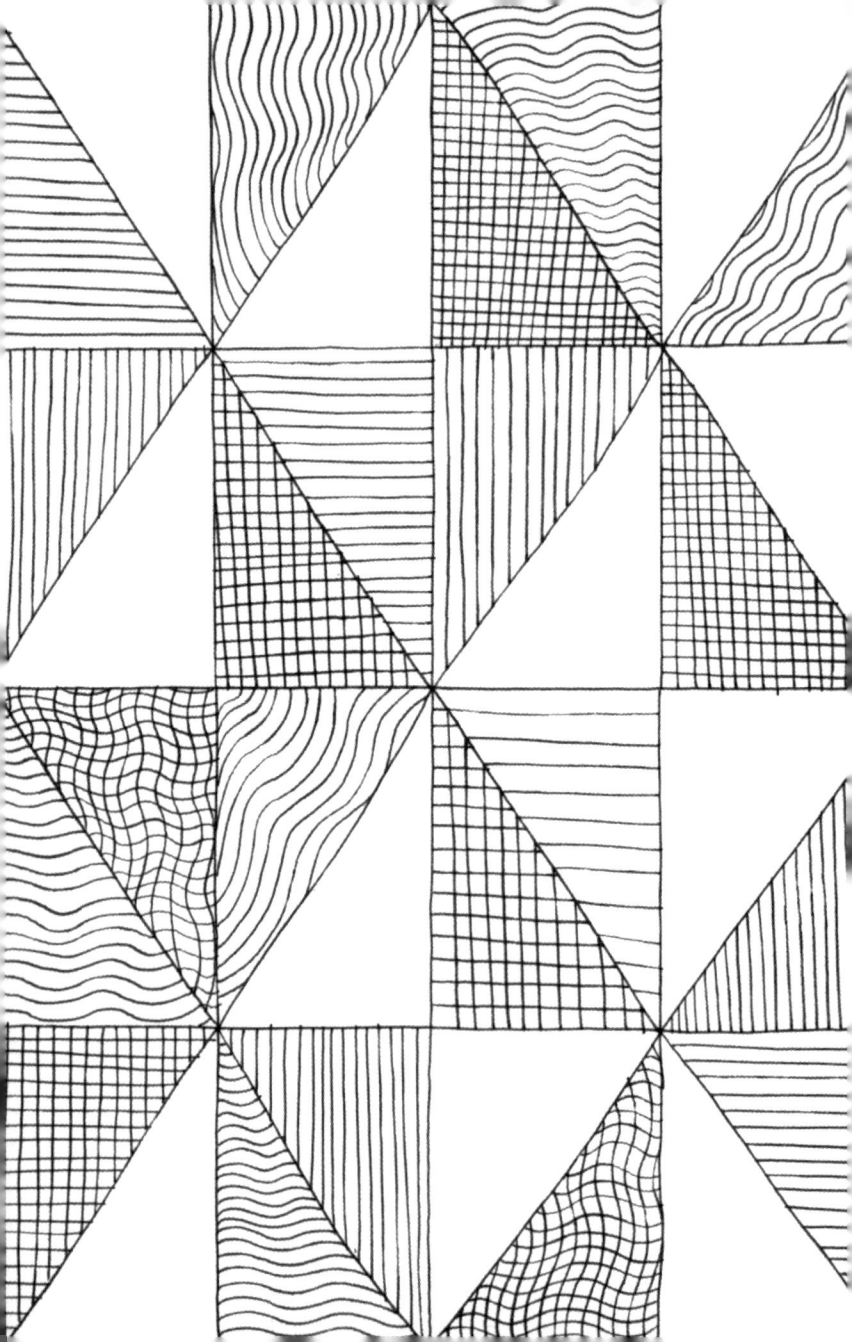

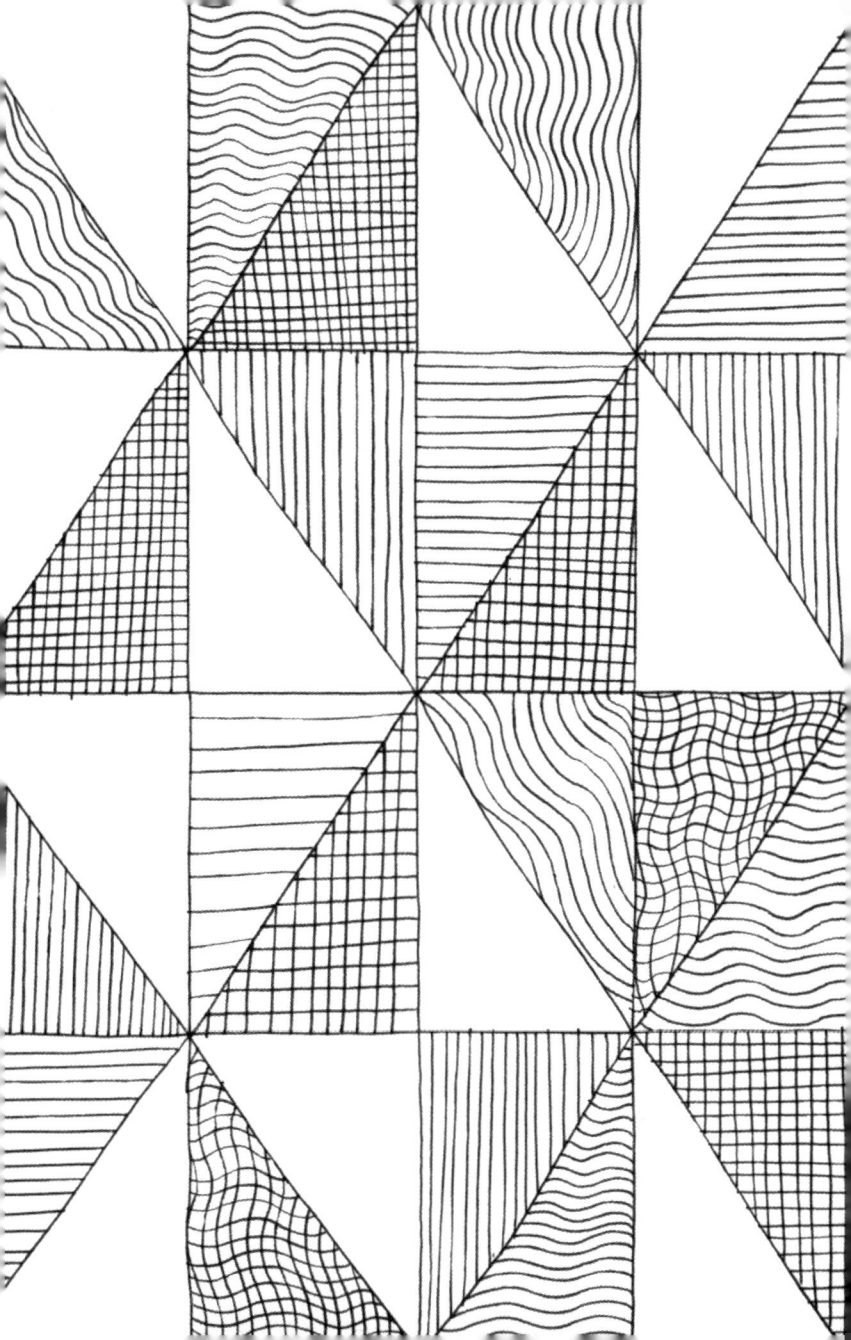

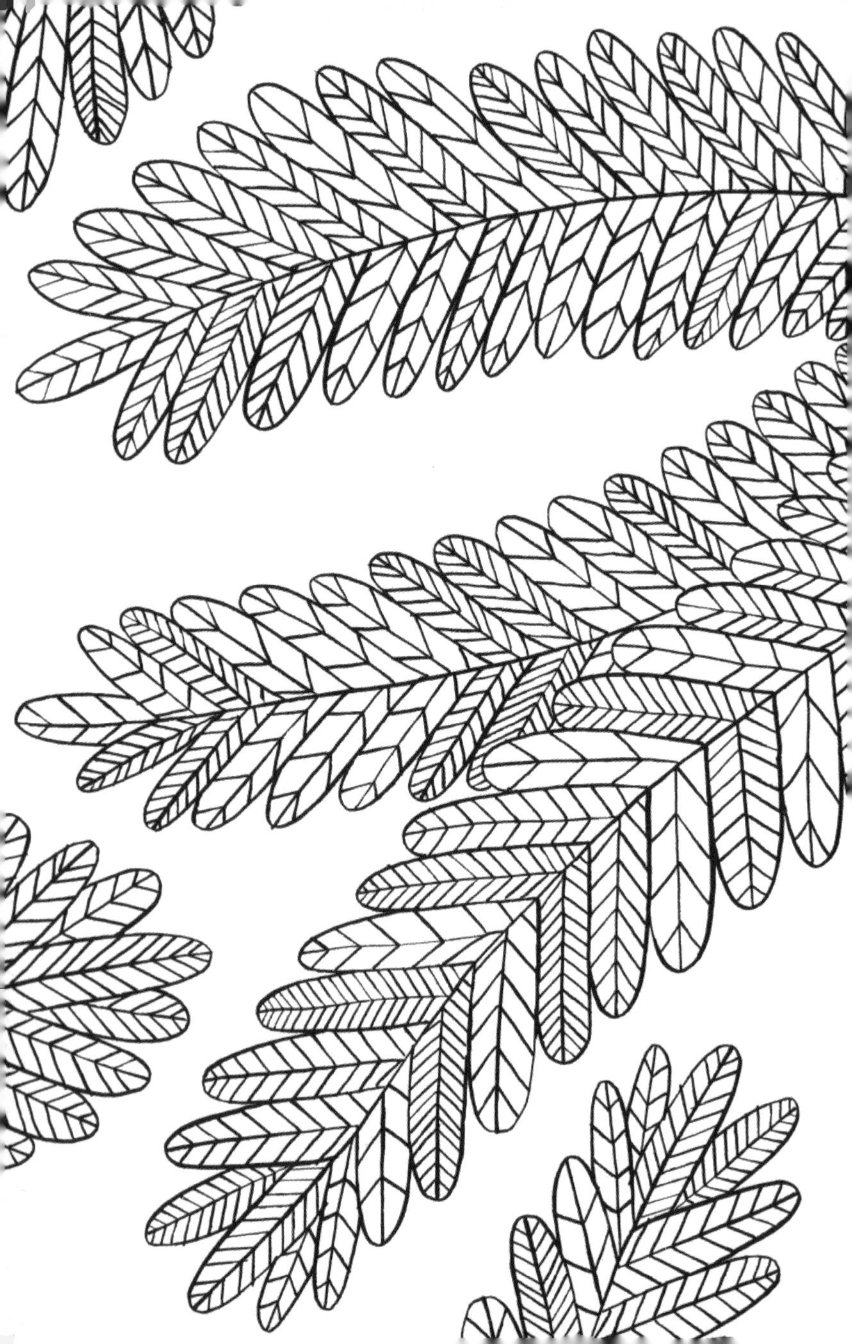

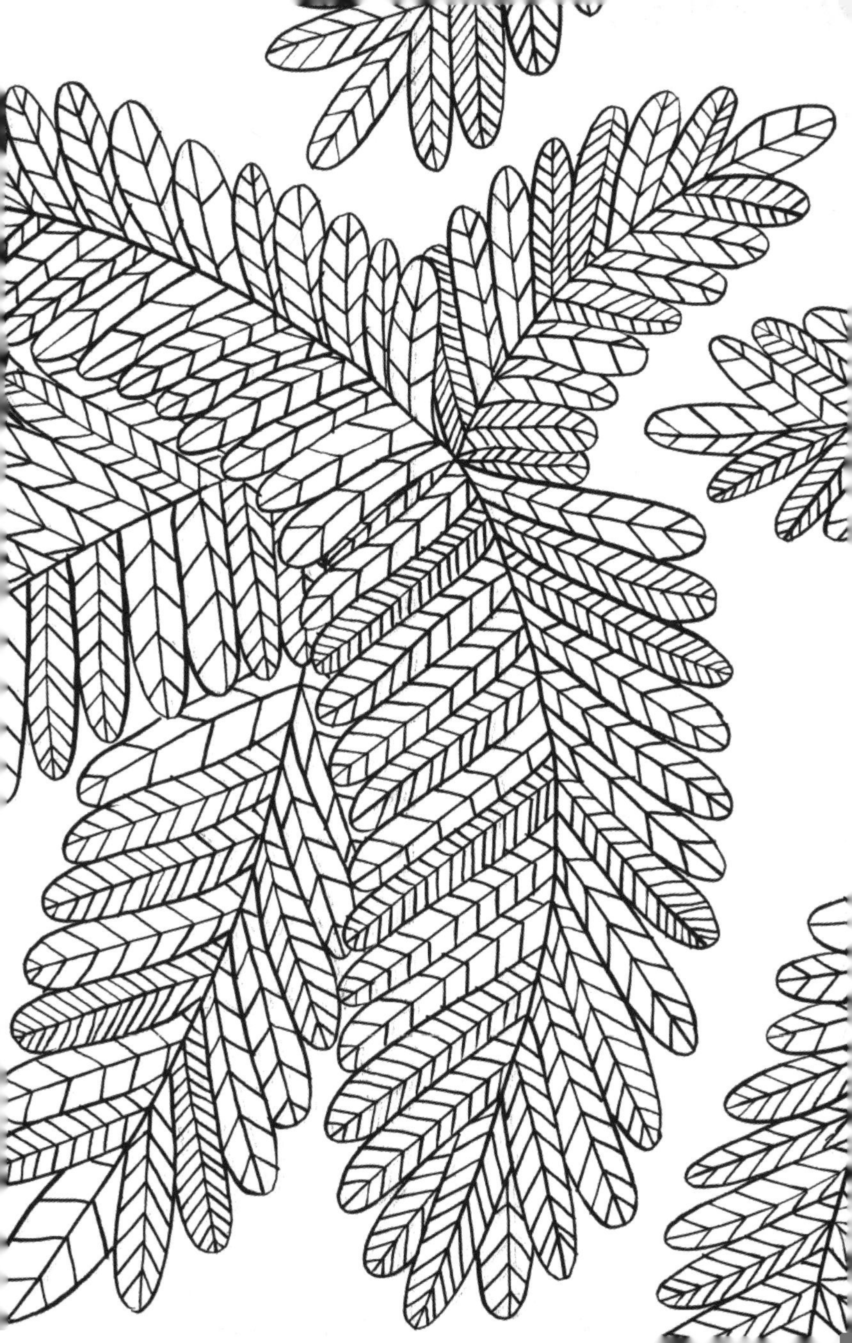

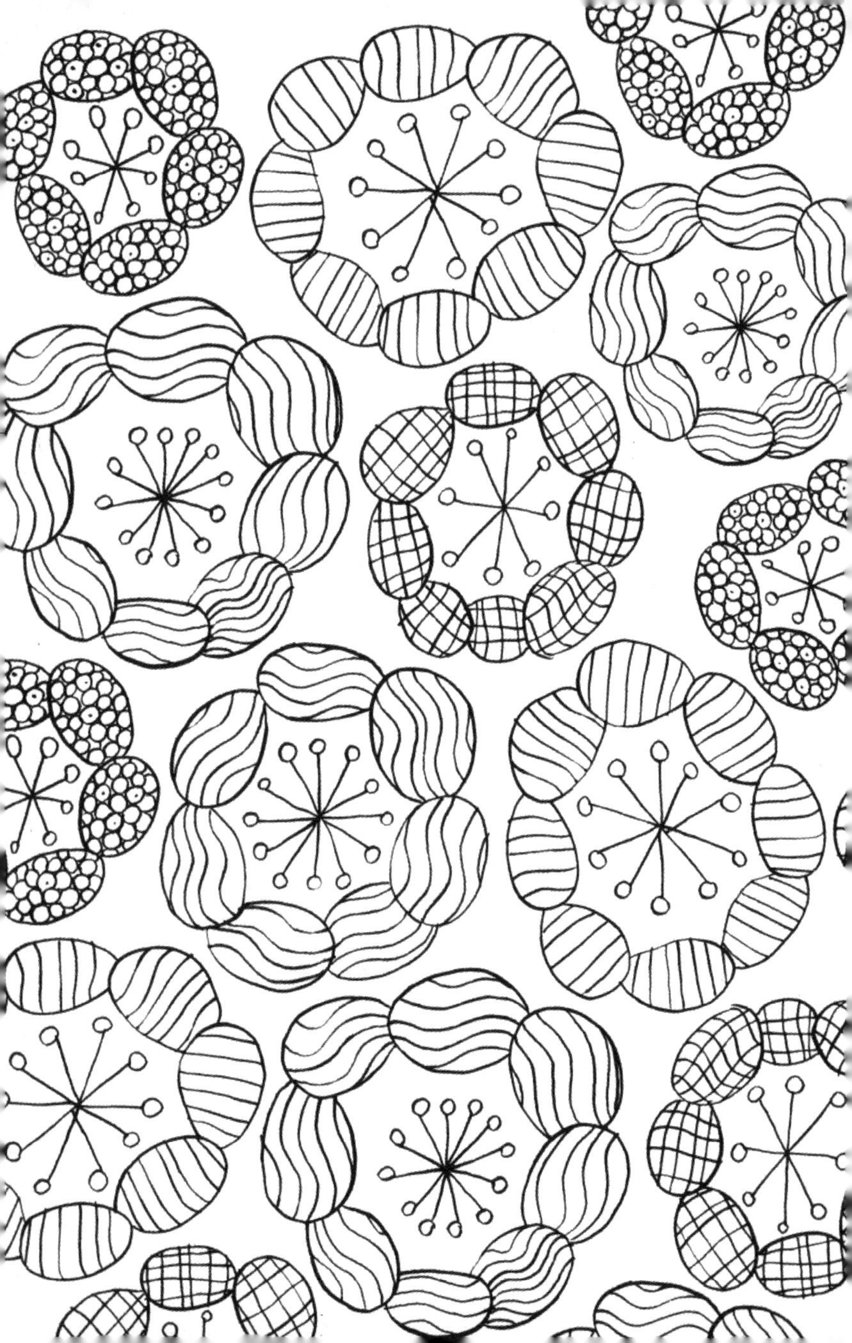

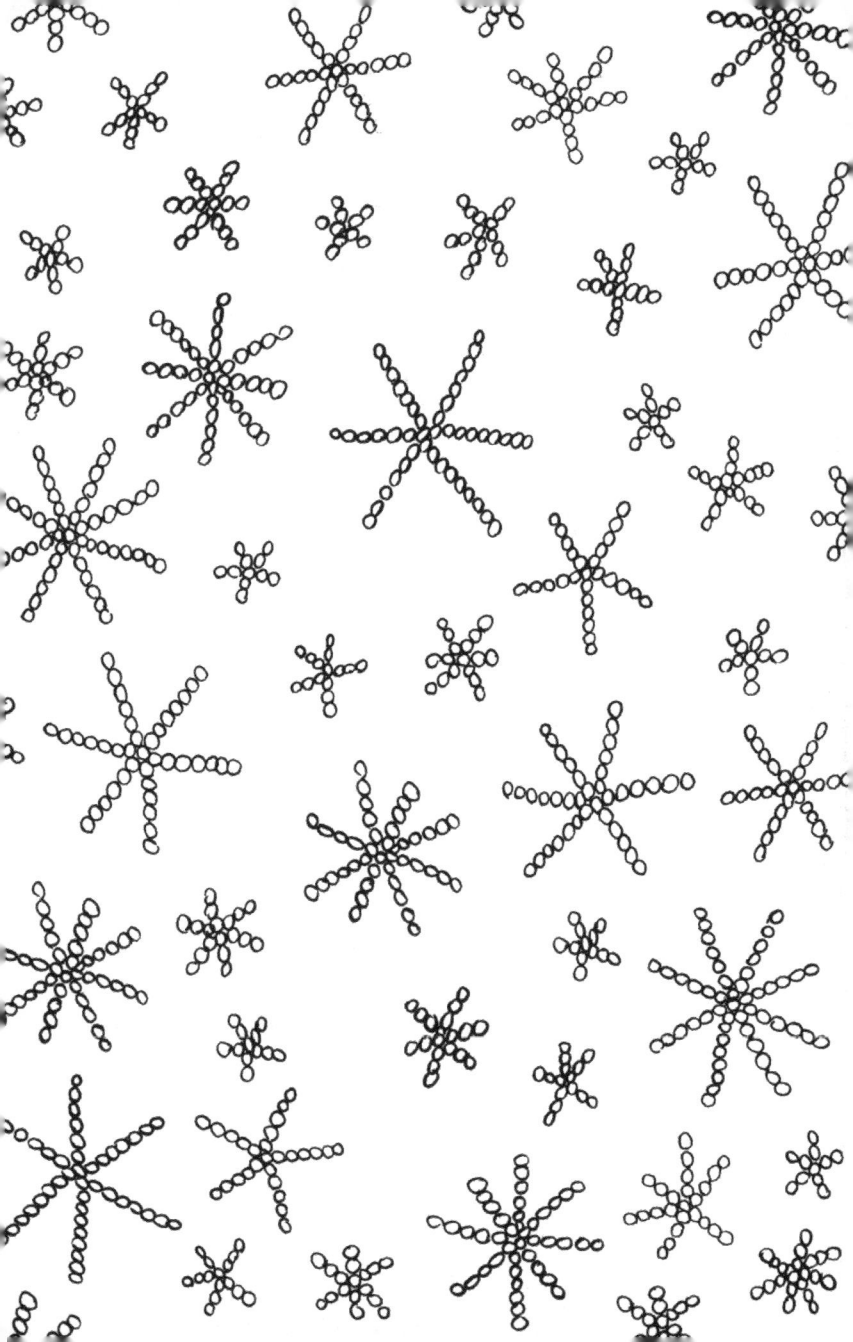

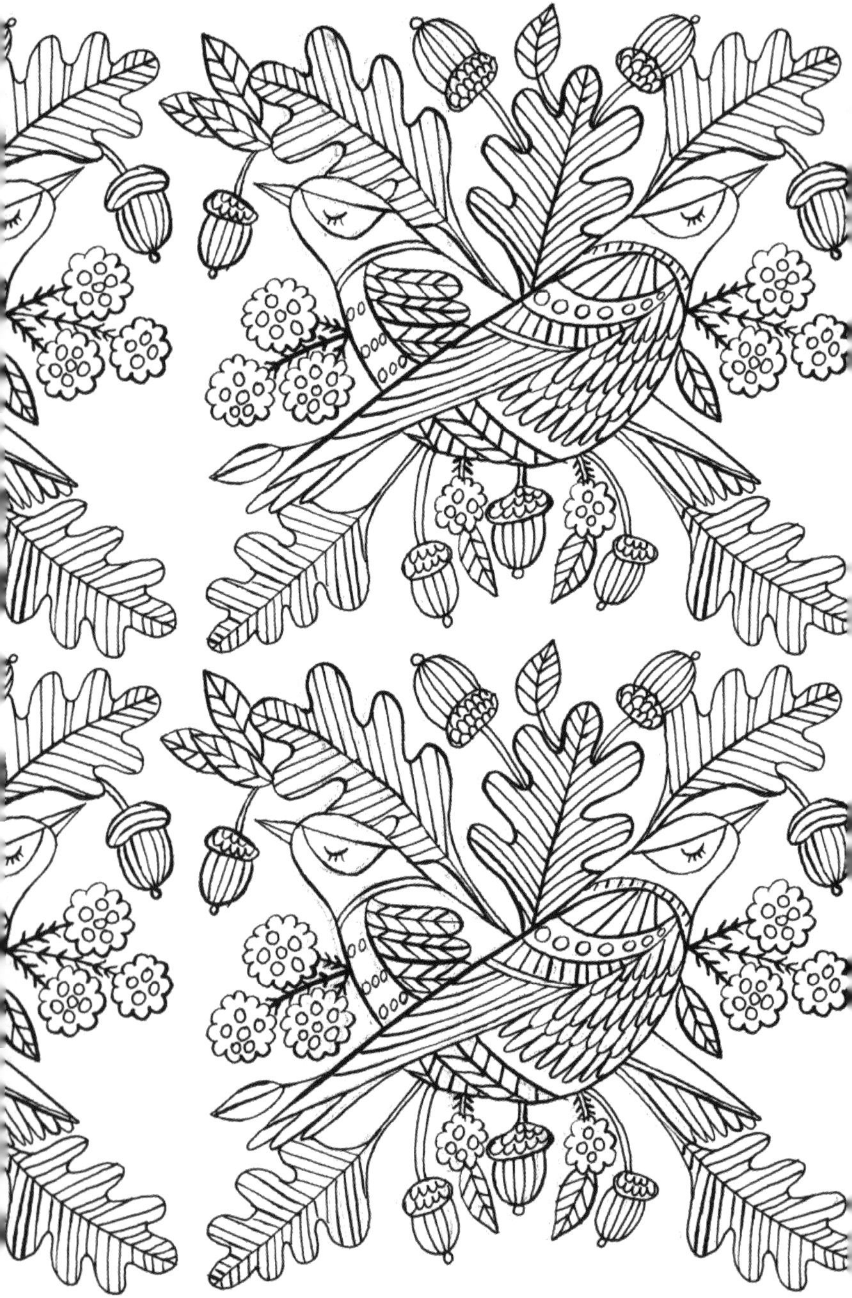

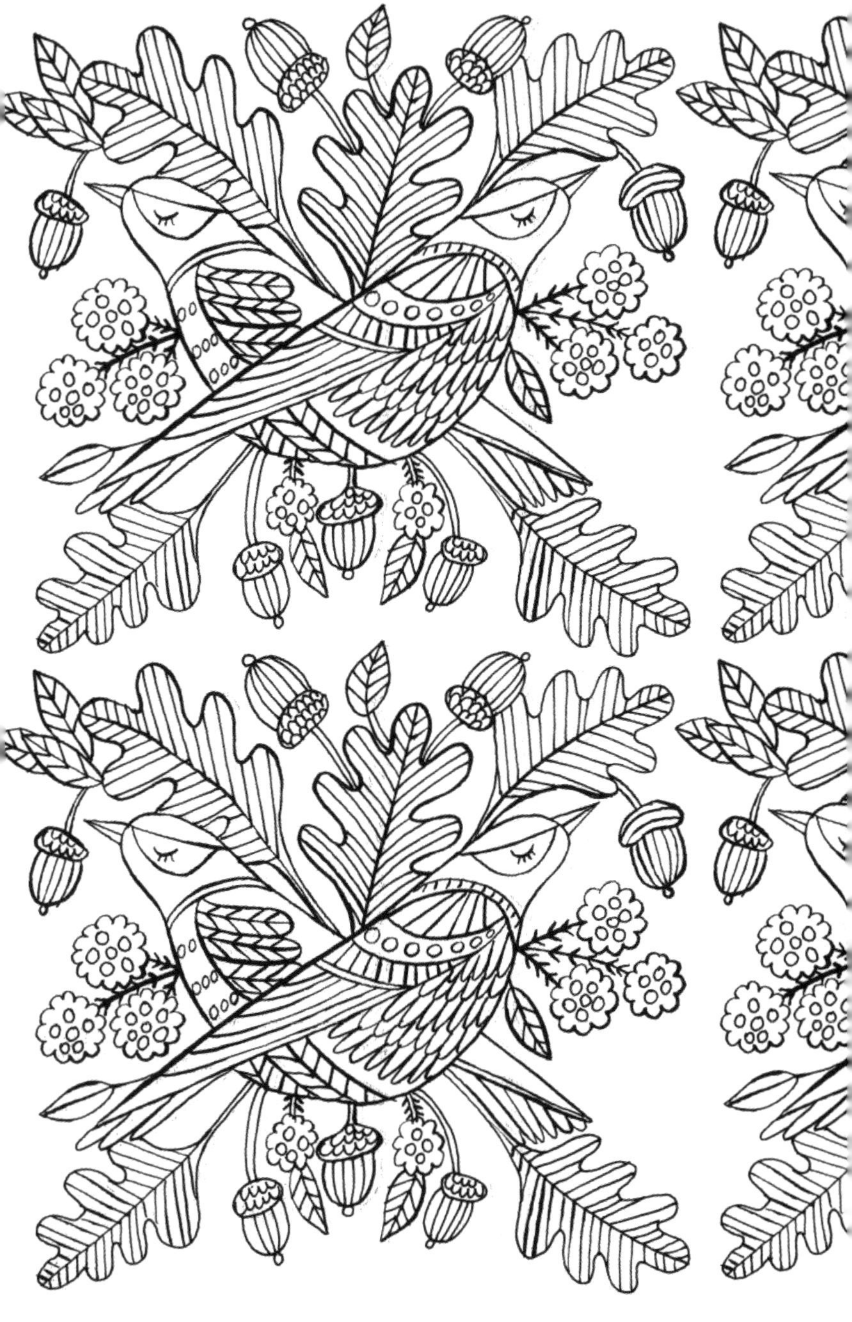

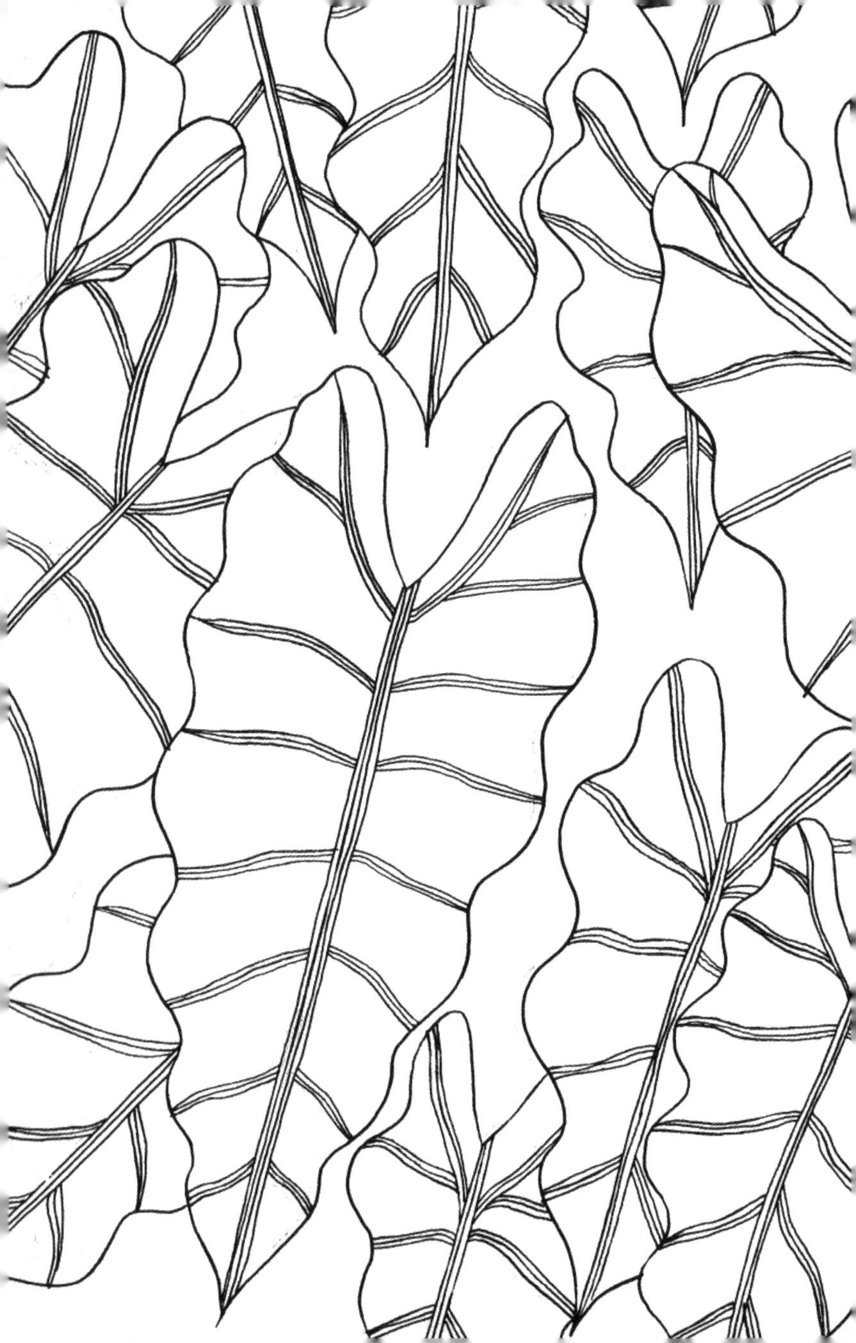

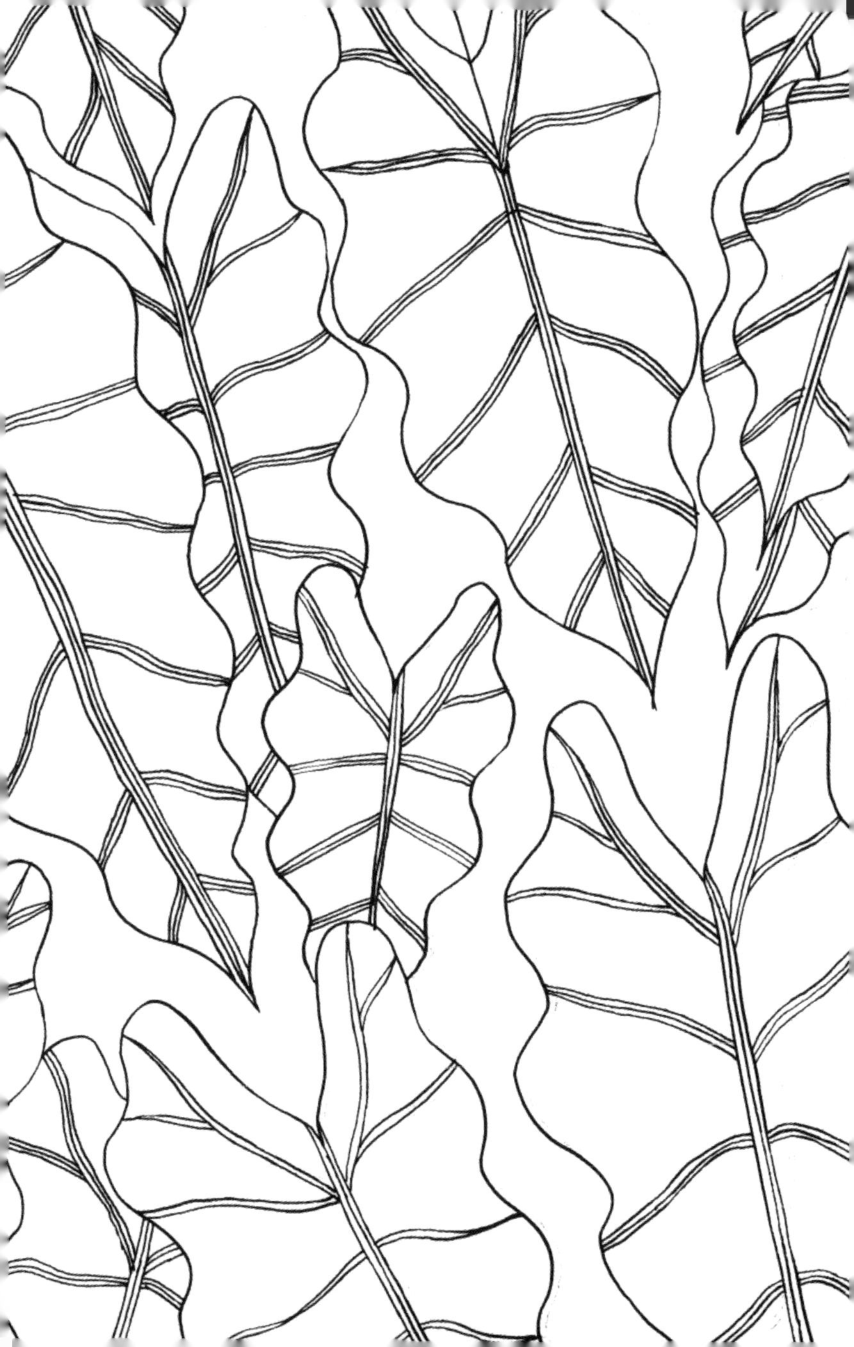

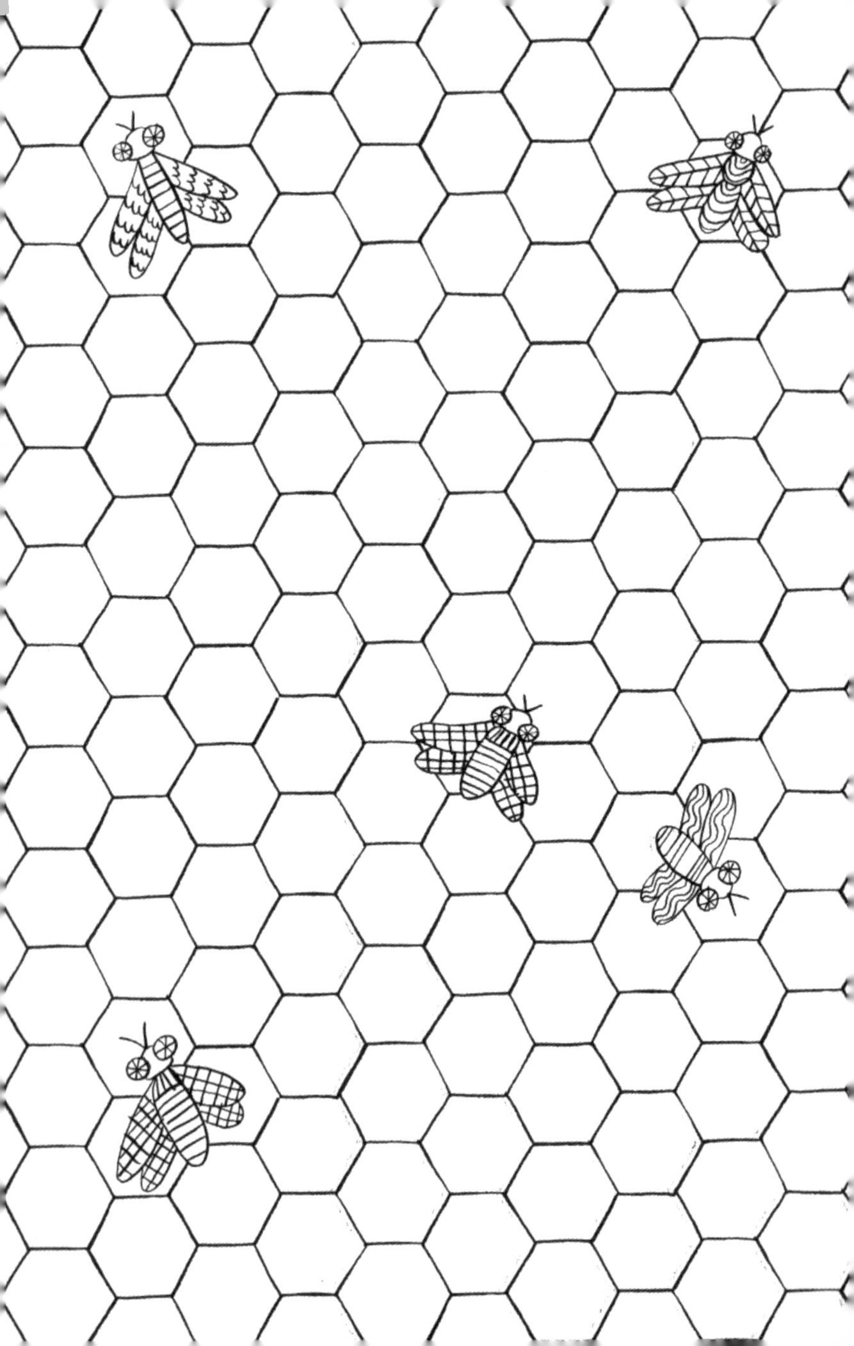

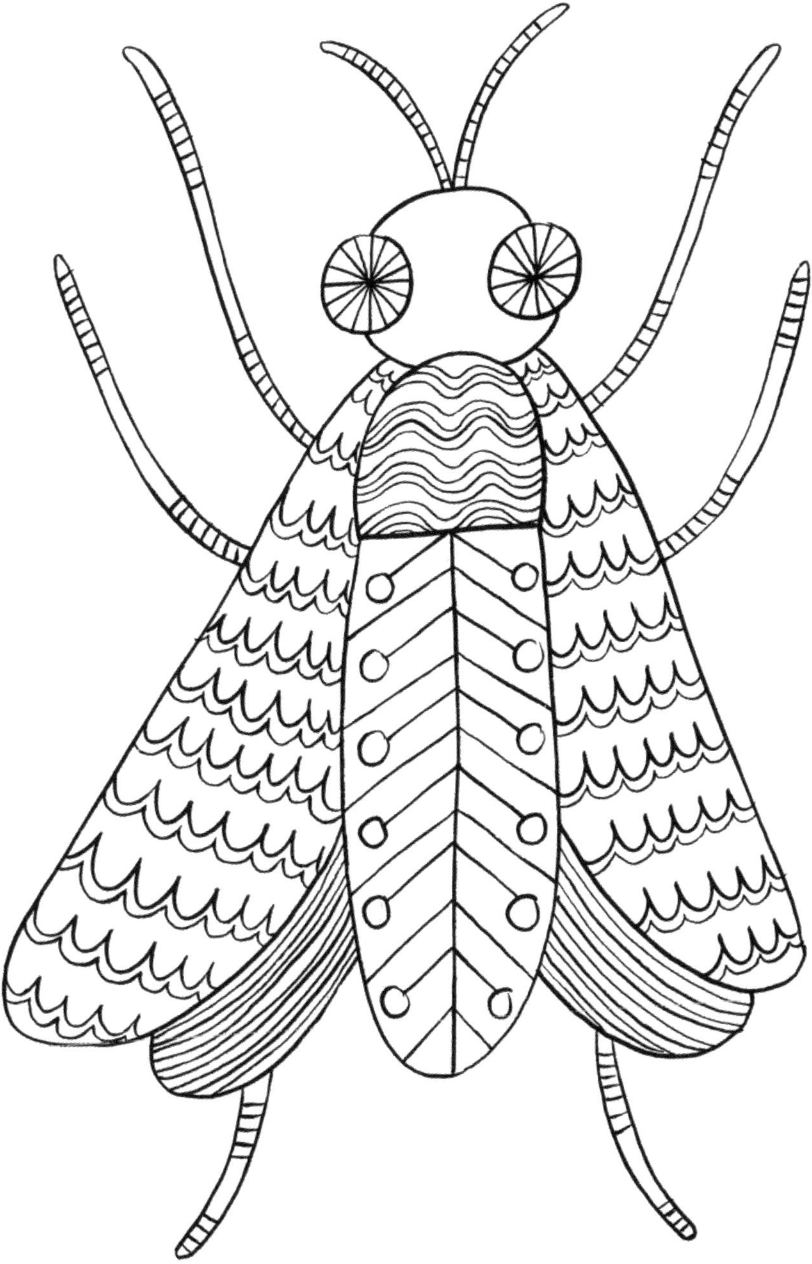

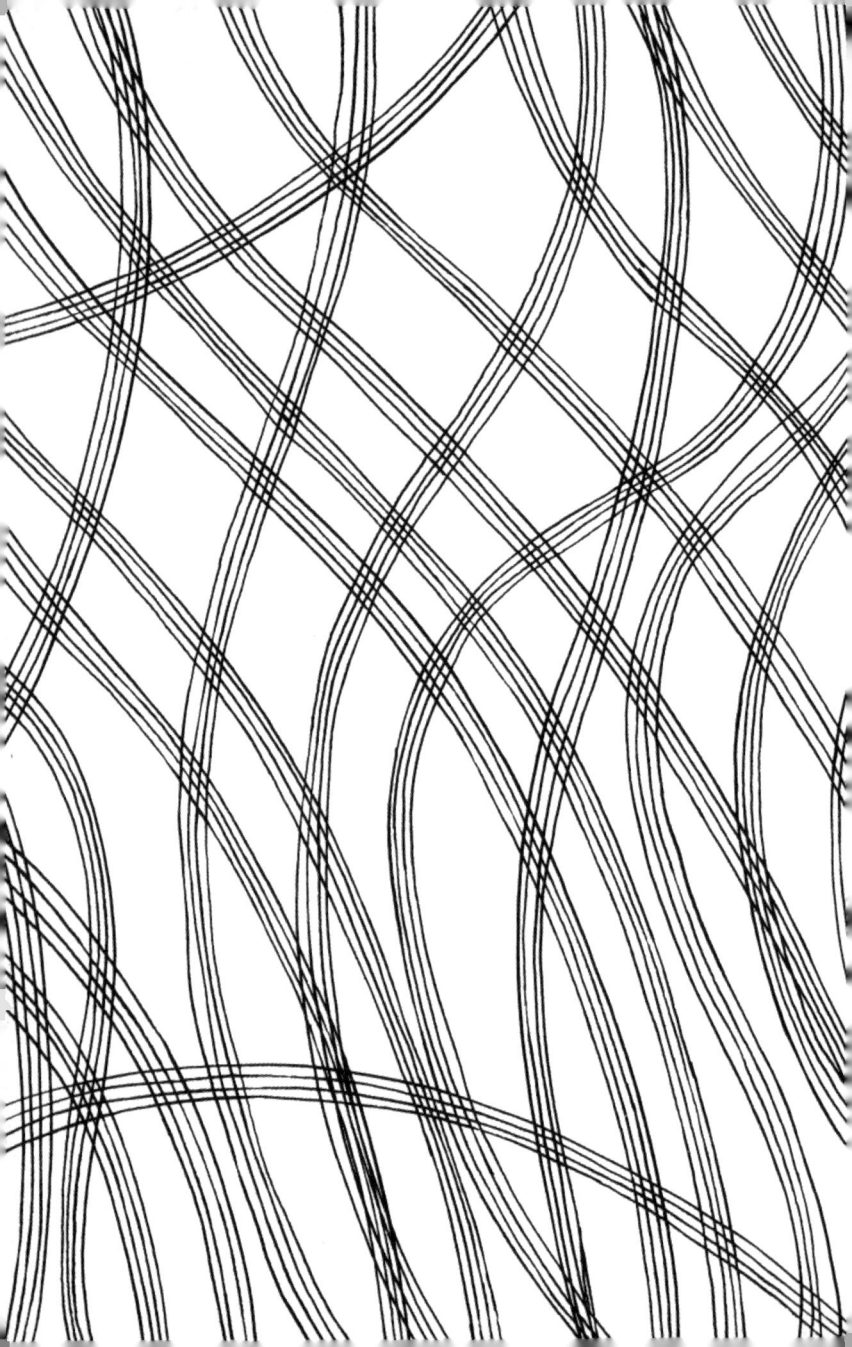

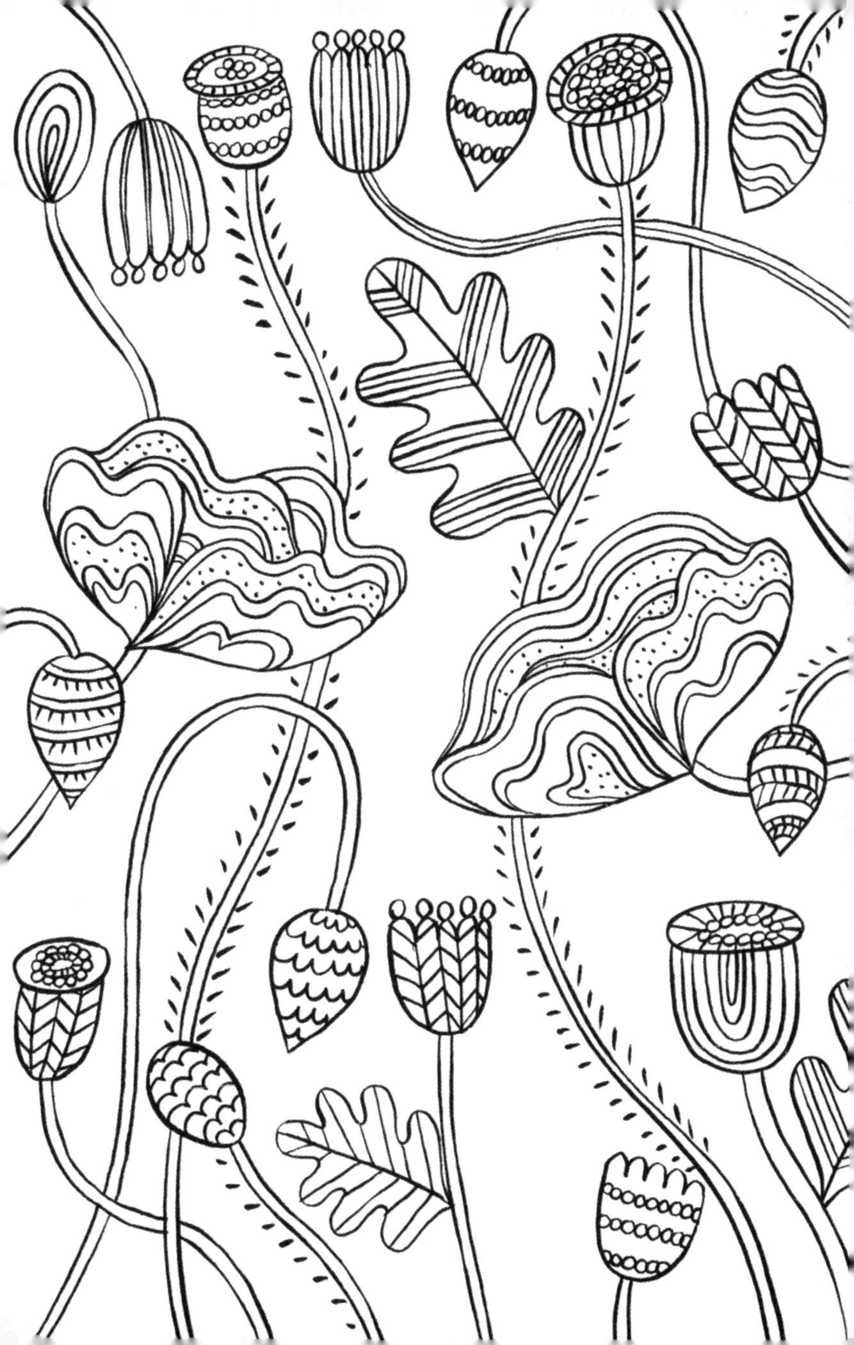

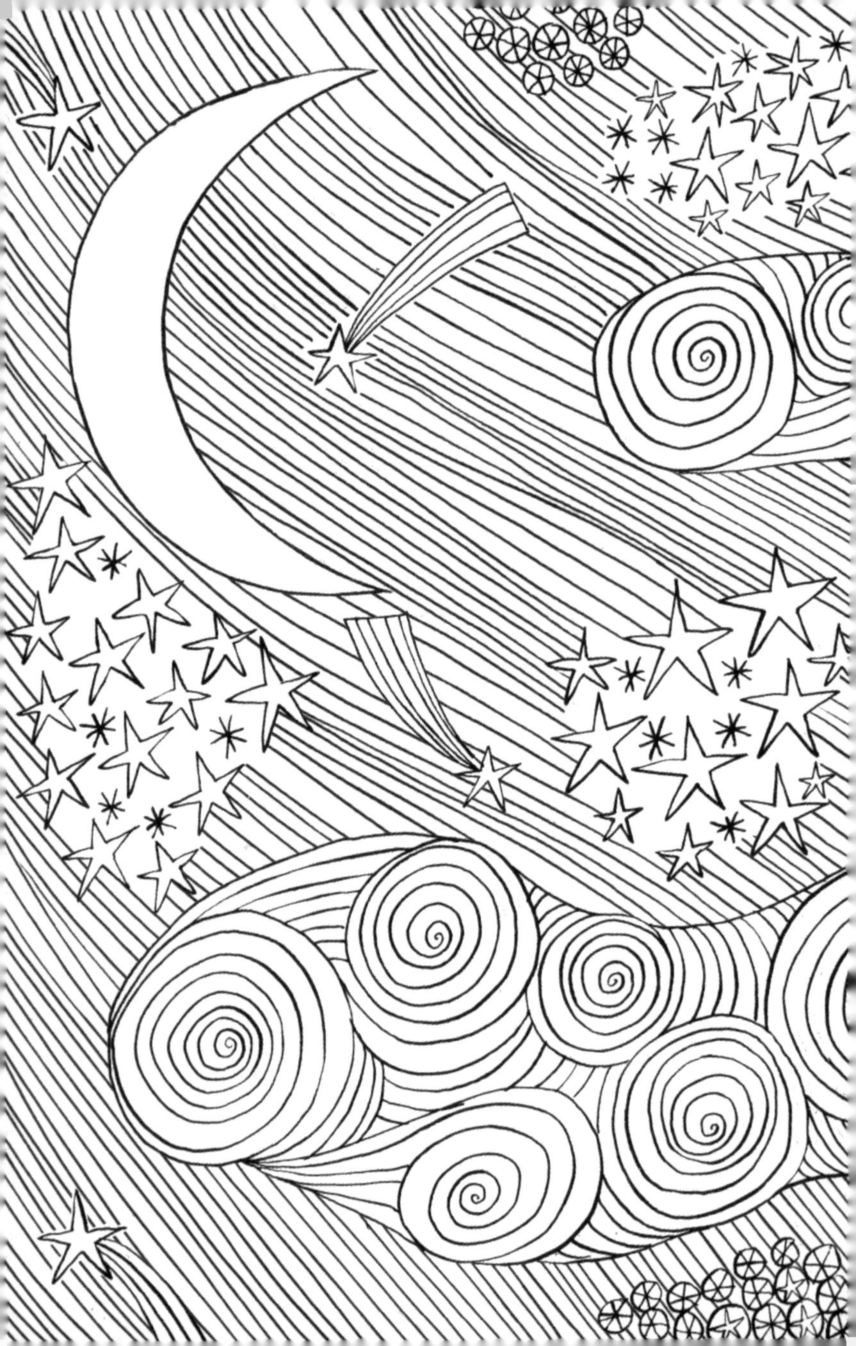

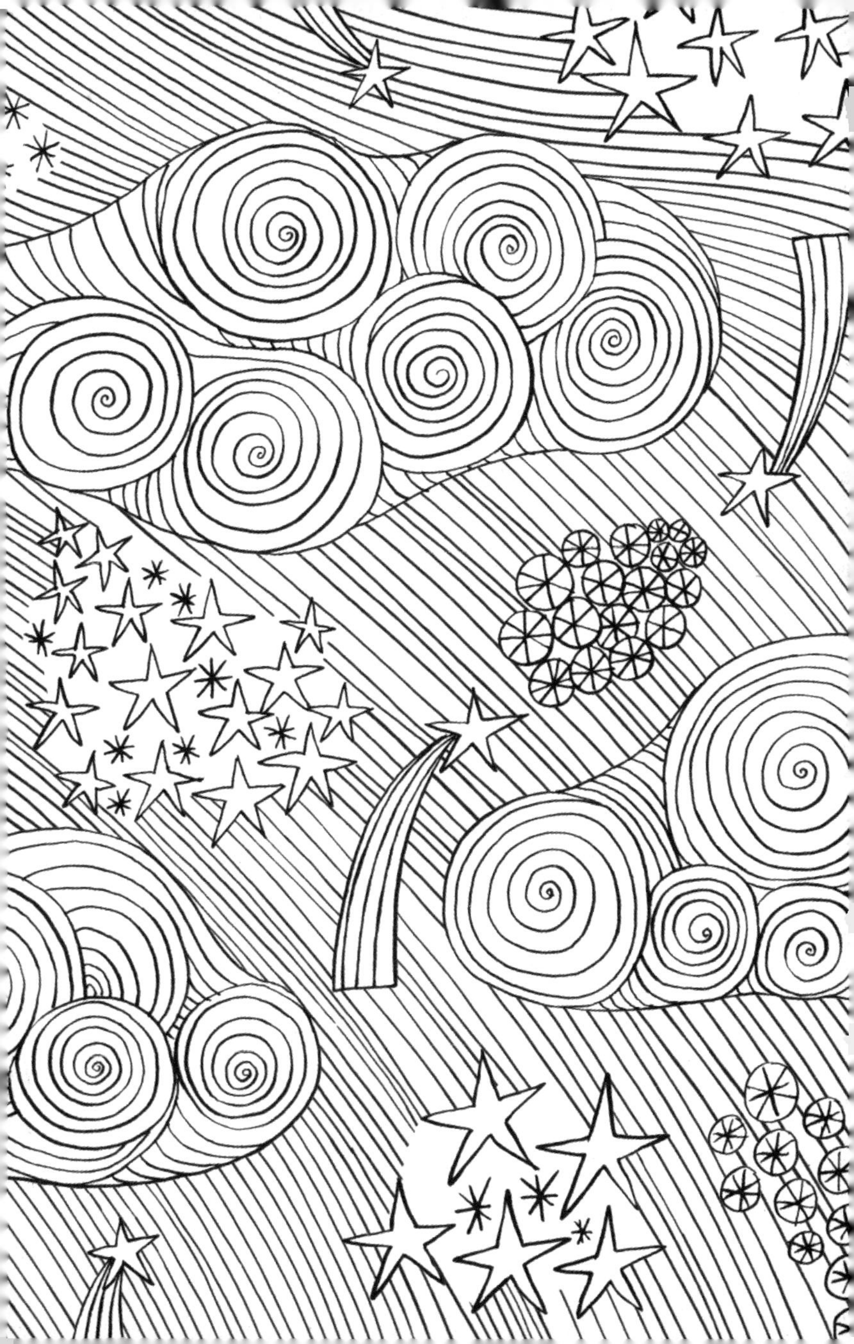

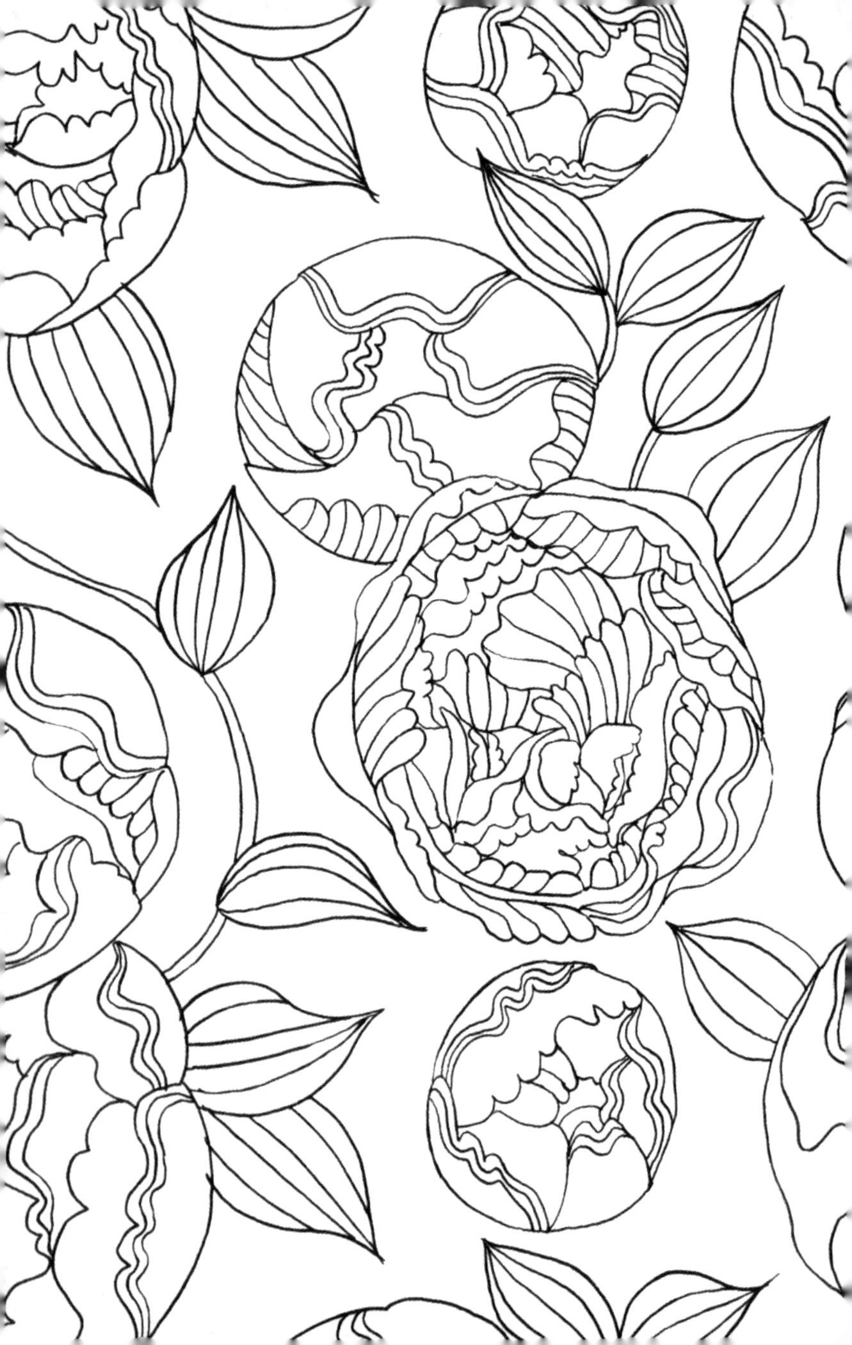

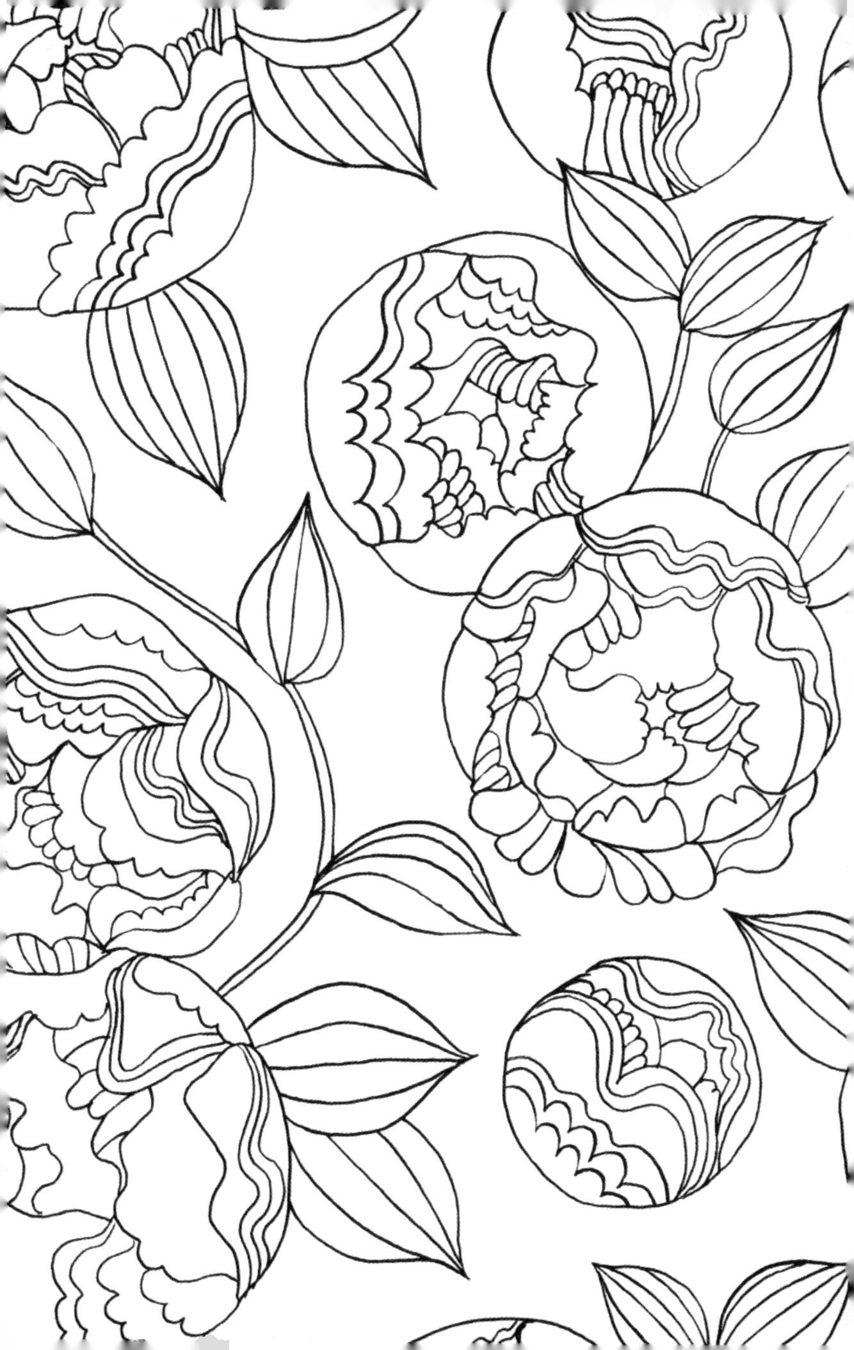

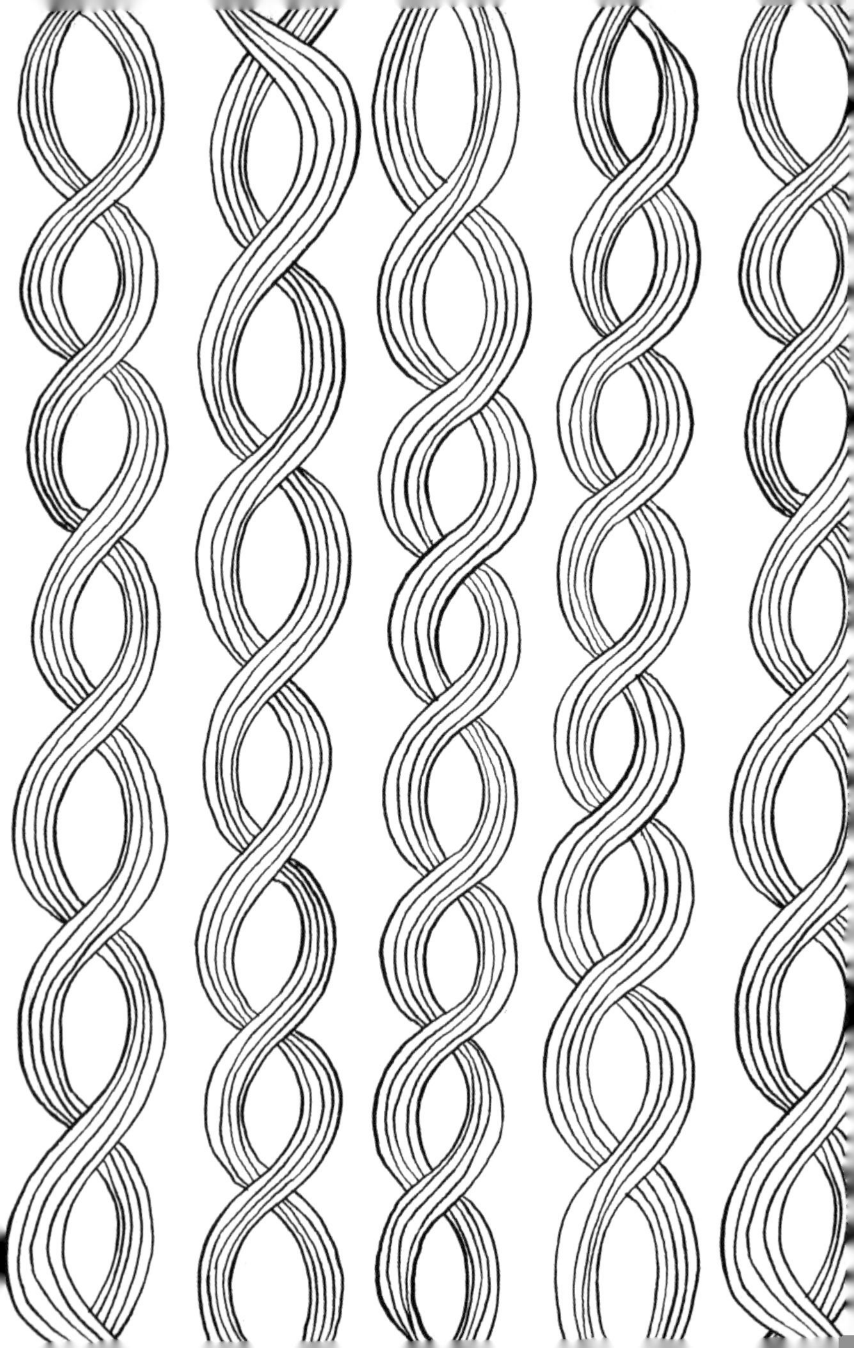

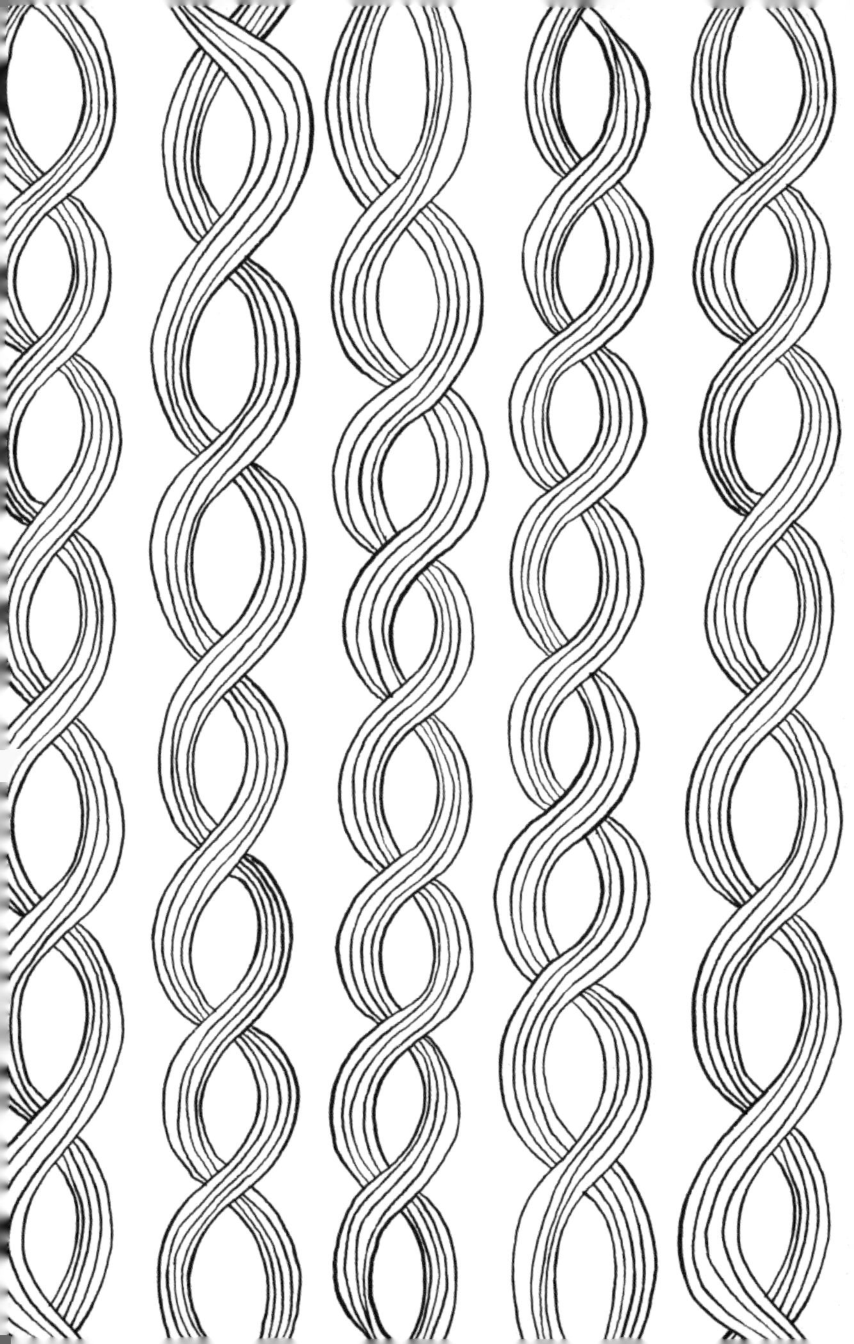

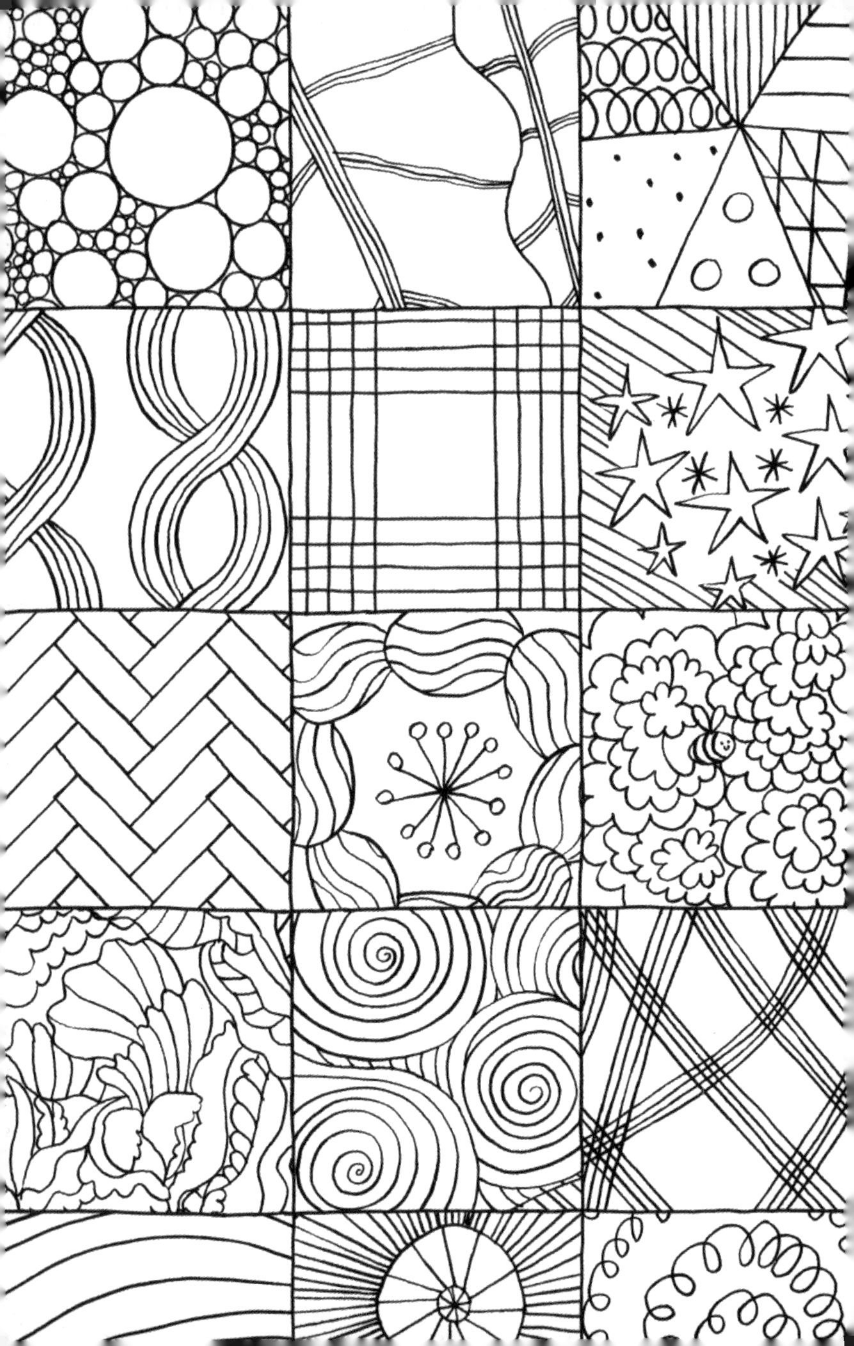

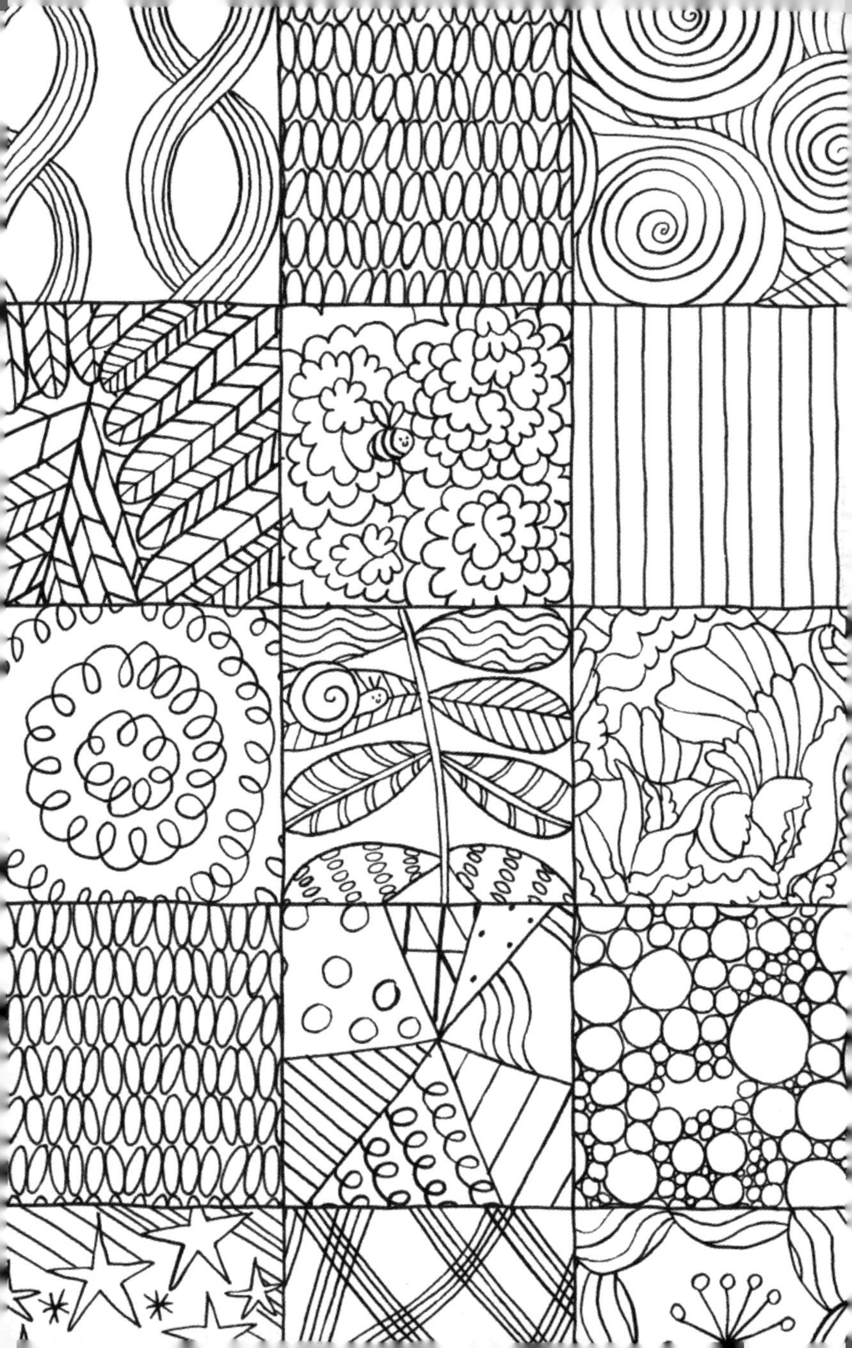

THANKS

I would like to thank Asger Bruun Jakobsen for cooking dinner for me those evenings I spent illustrating my mindful patterns.

A special thank you to my textile teacher, Lisa, for opening my eyes to the world of lines, pattern repeat and the versatility of potato printing.

A big thank you to everyone who coloured my first book.

EMMA FARRARONS
illustration & art direction

www.emmafarrarons.com

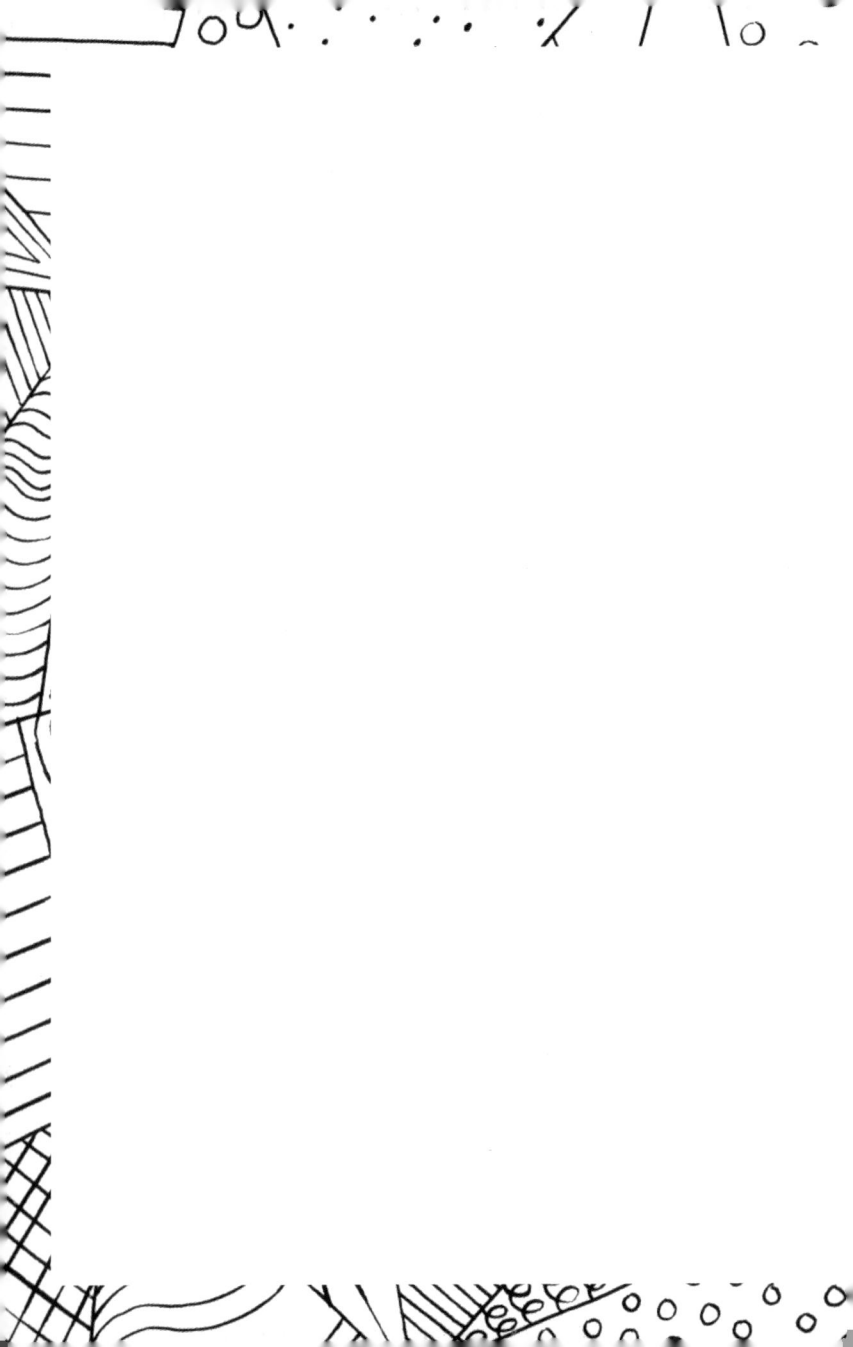

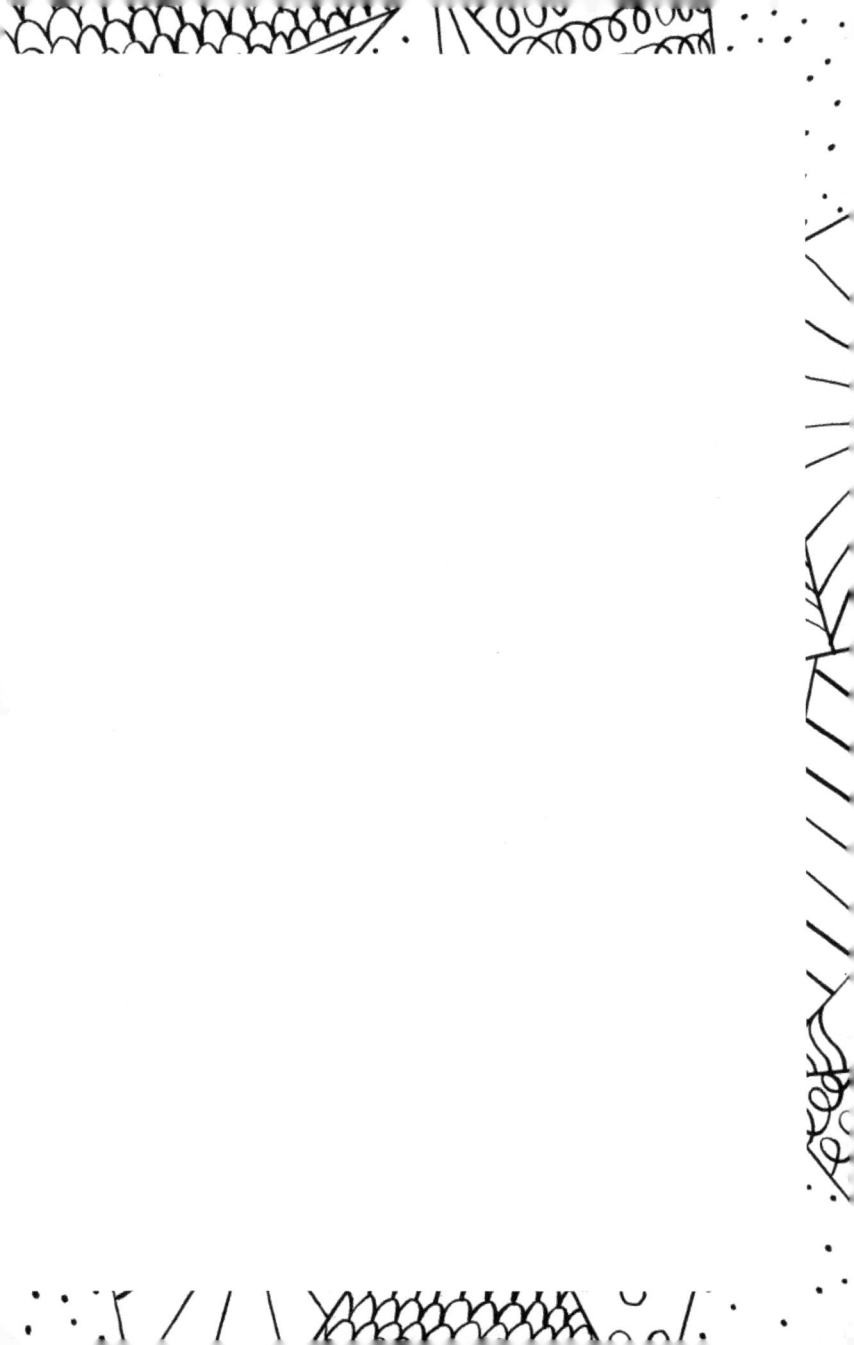

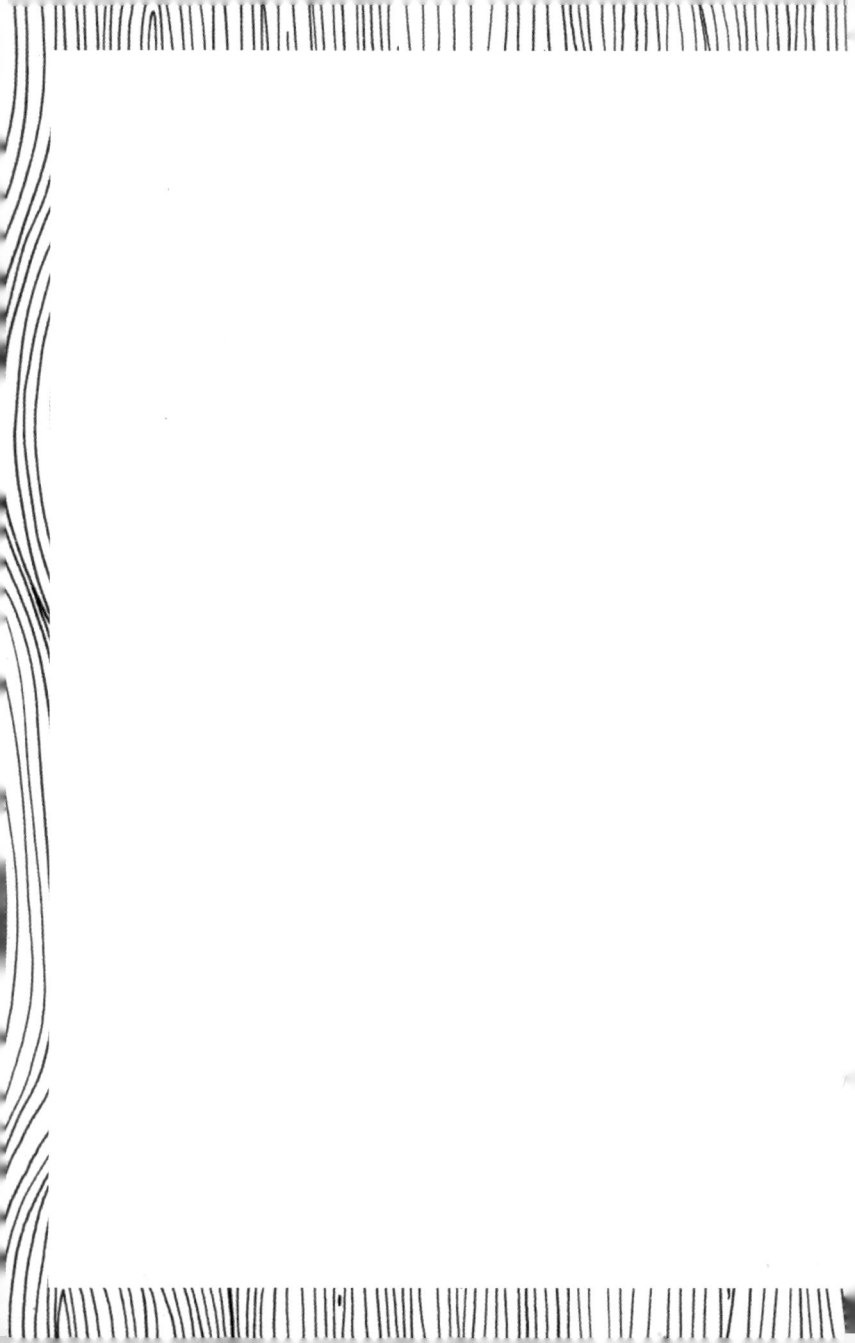

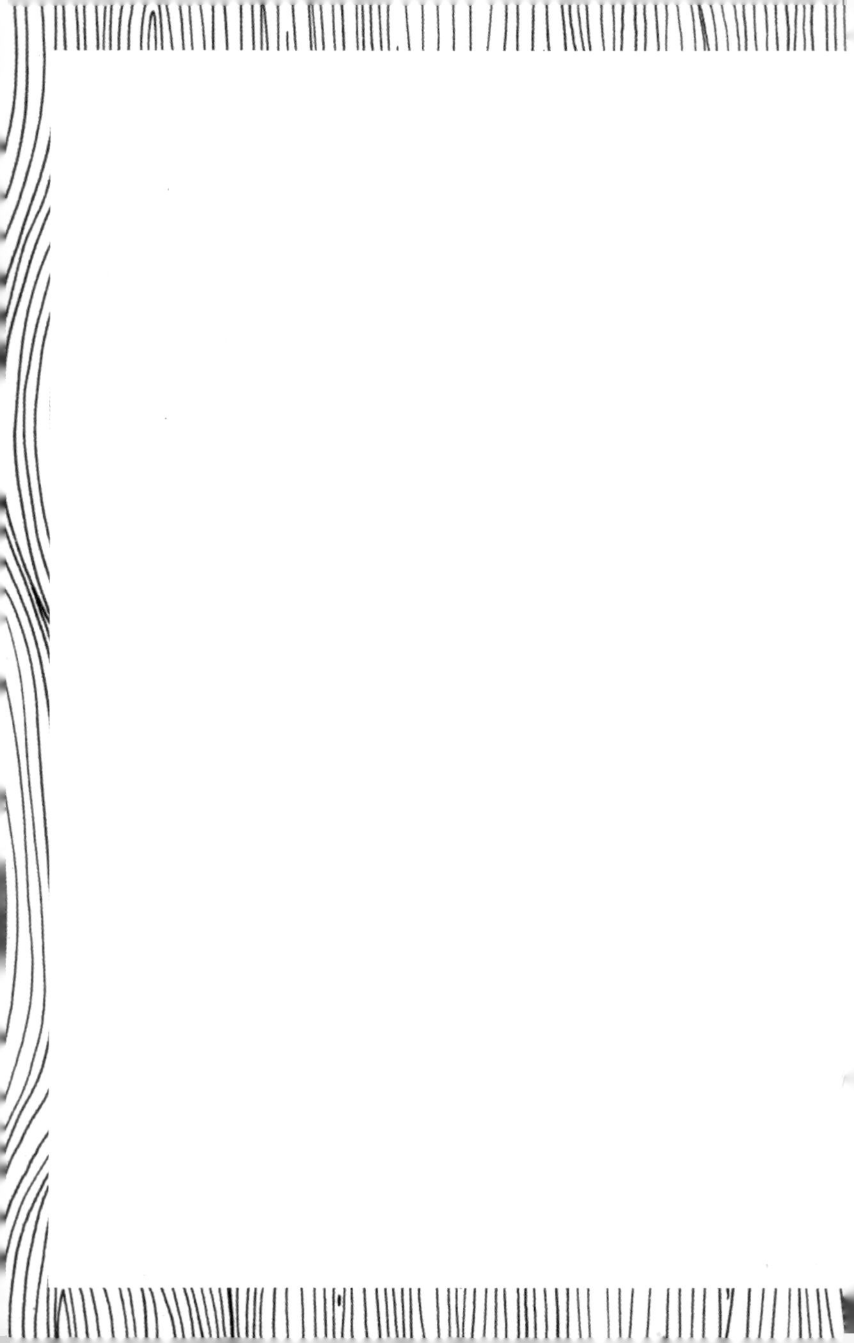